Seascapes & Landscapes

Chris Coles

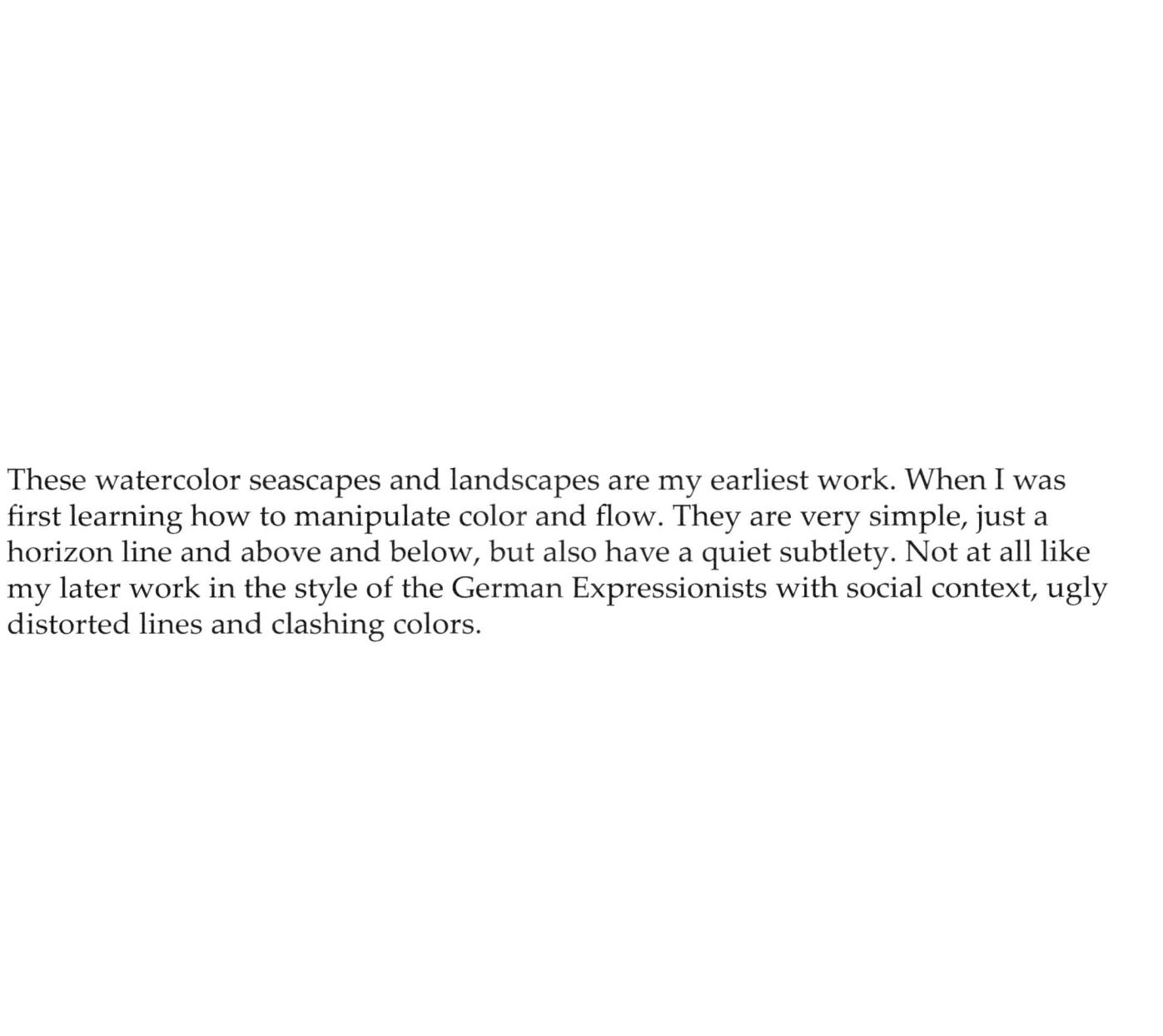

These watercolor seascapes and landscapes are my earliest work. When I was first learning how to manipulate color and flow. They are very simple, just a horizon line and above and below, but also have a quiet subtlety. Not at all like my later work in the style of the German Expressionists with social context, ugly distorted lines and clashing colors.

Dawn Light Penobscot Bay

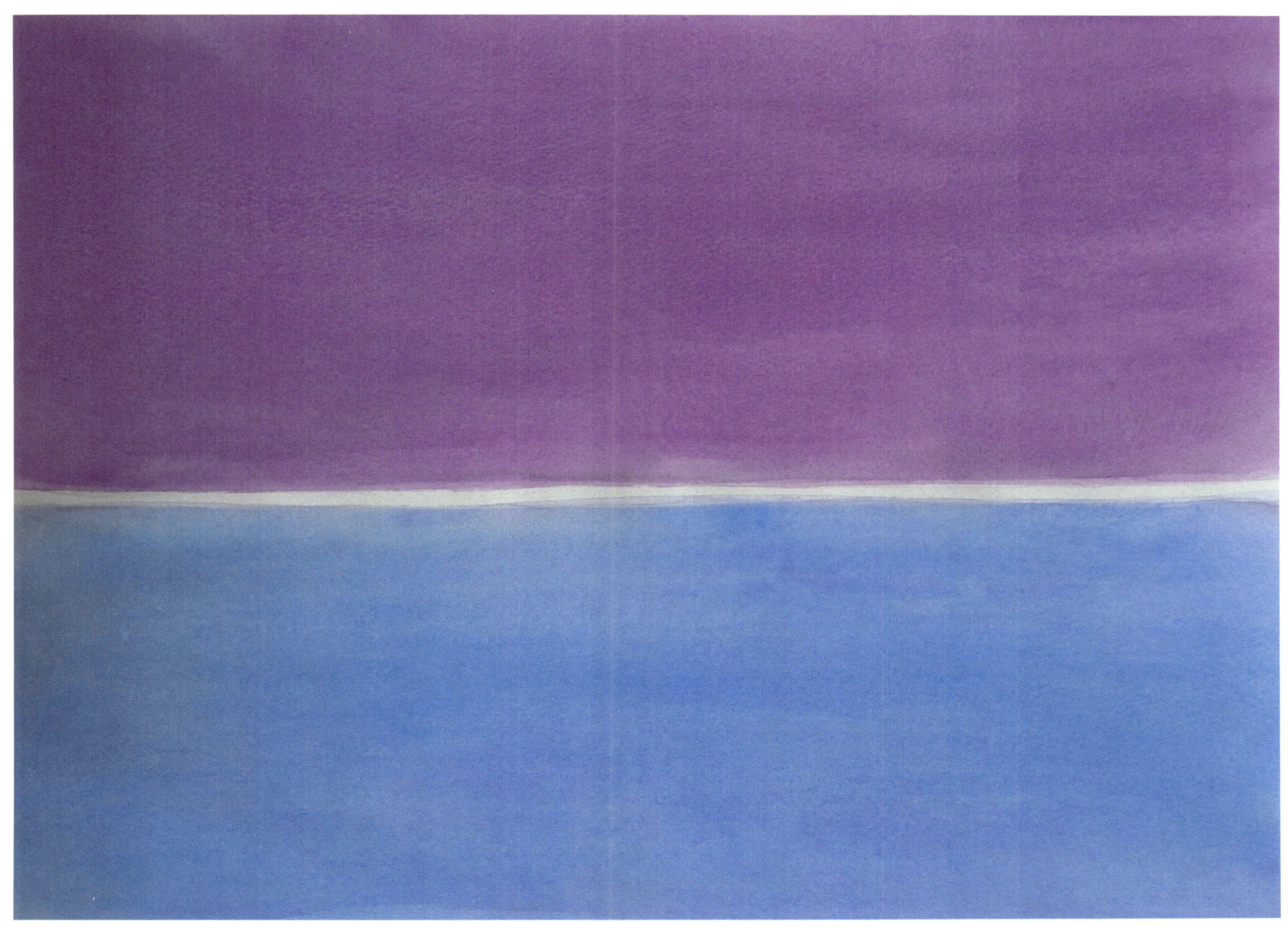

Before Dawn Penobscot Bay

Purple Dusk Andaman Sea

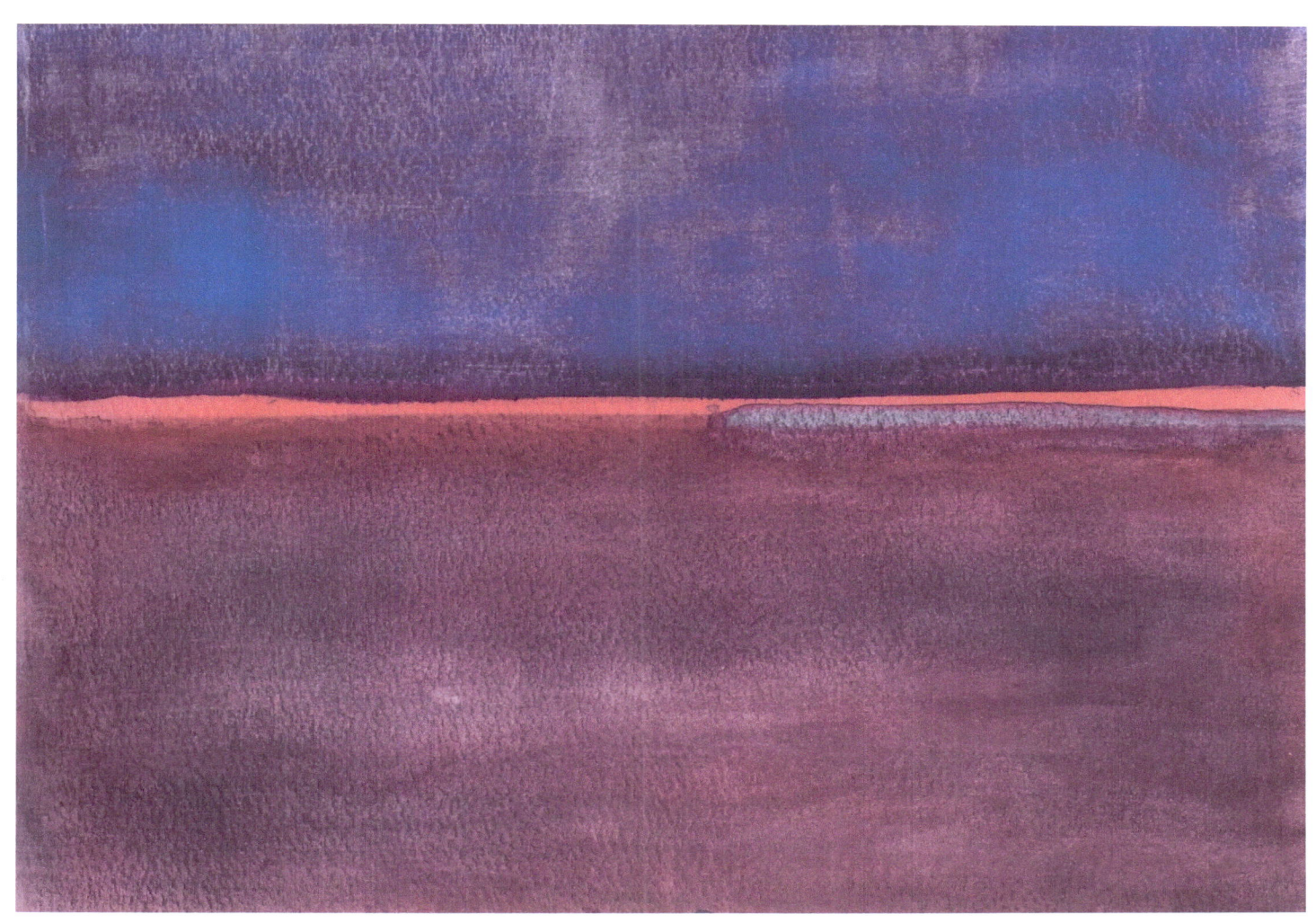

Andaman Sea Dusk

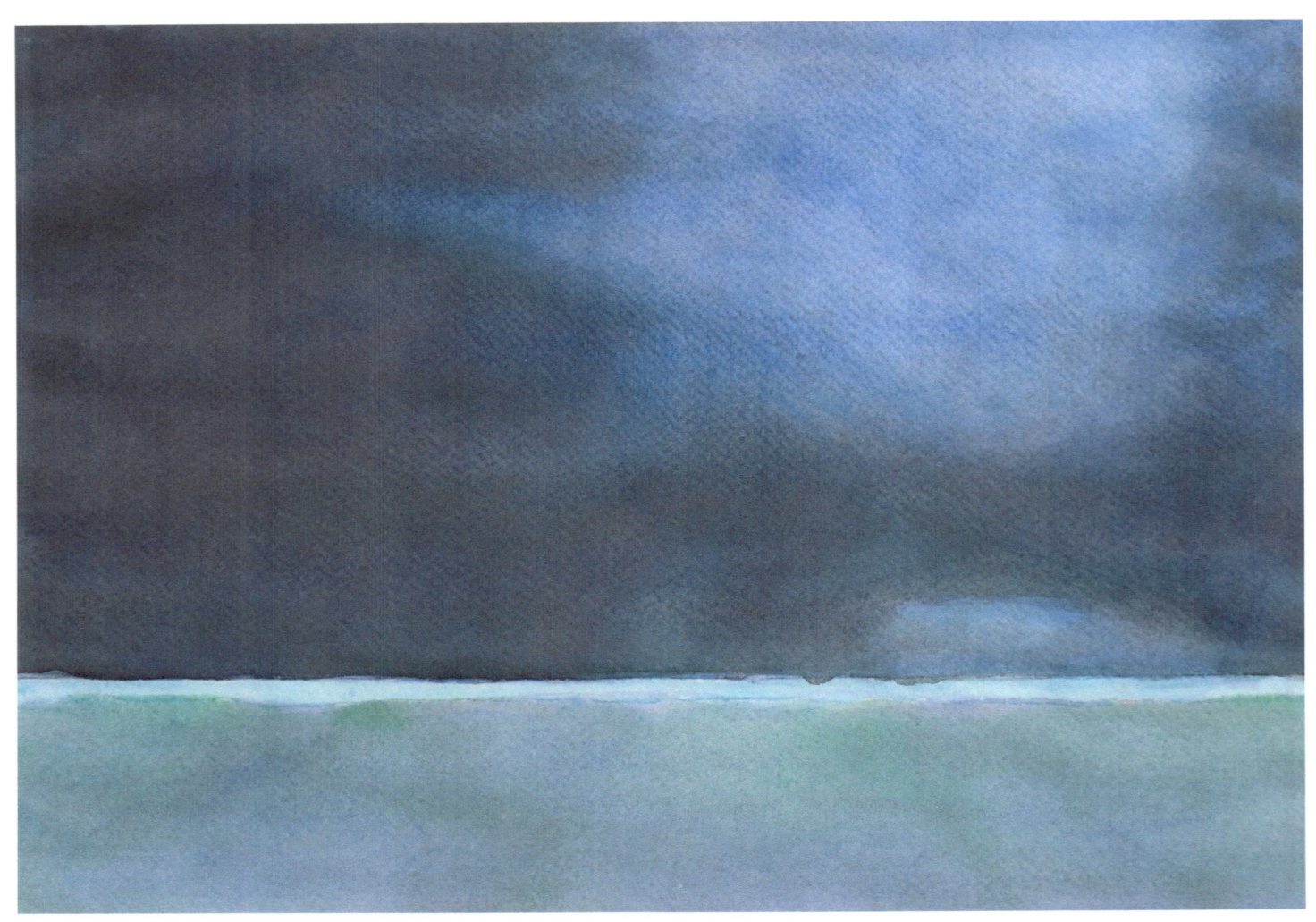

Monsoon Squall Approaching Phuket

Rain Over the Andaman Sea

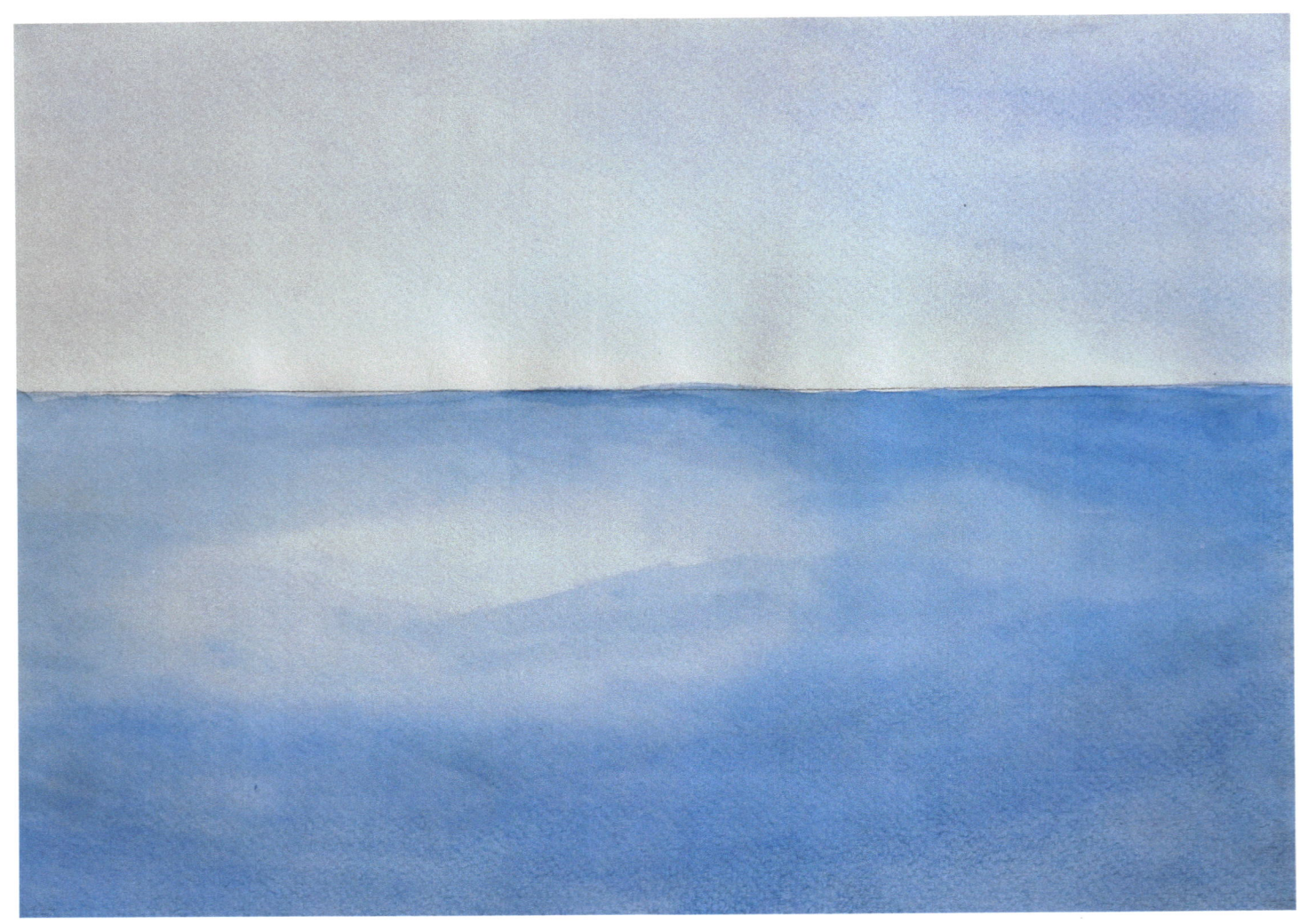

Approaching Criehaven Penobscot Bay

Upper Penobscot Bay

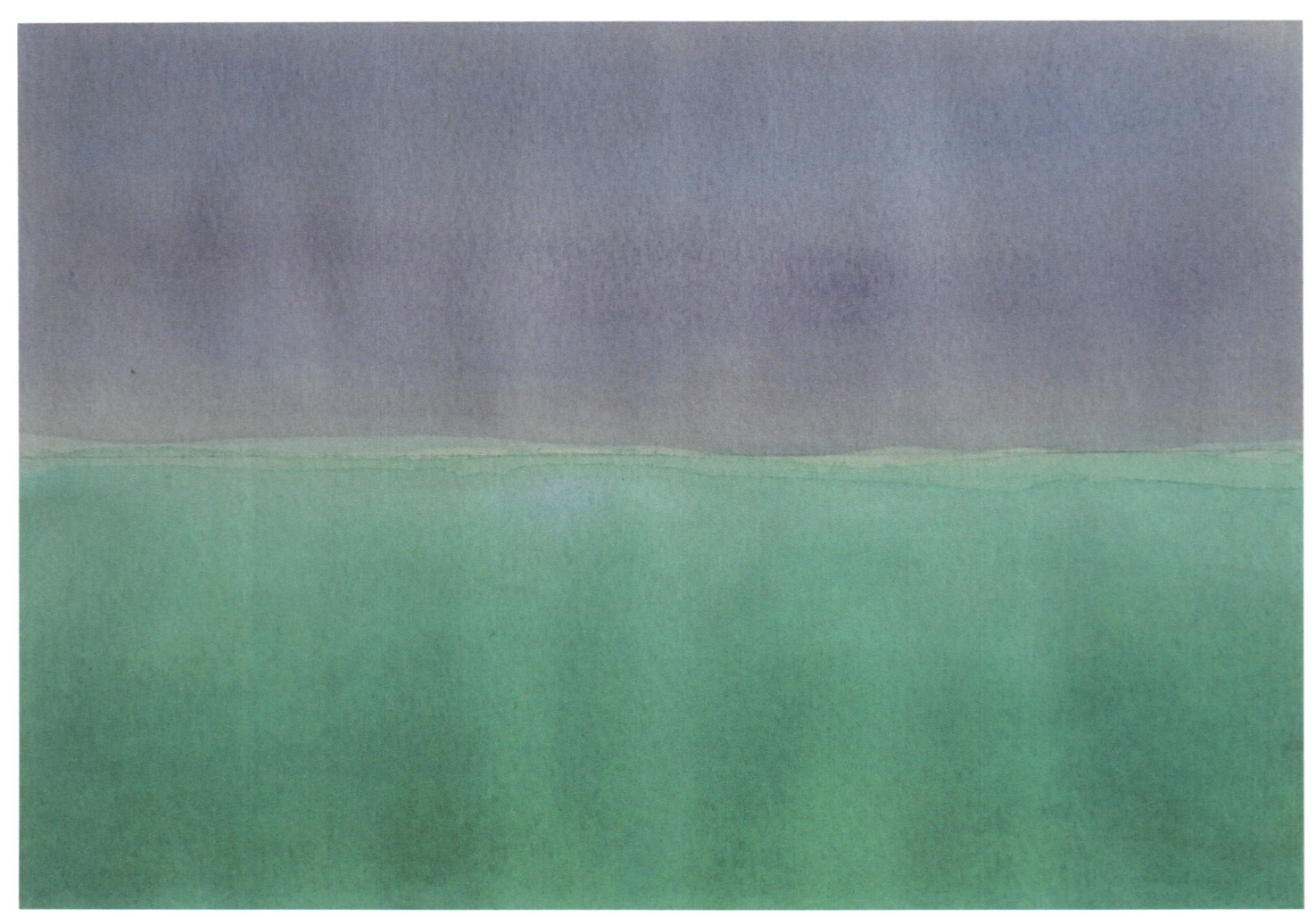

Koh Tao Southern Thailand

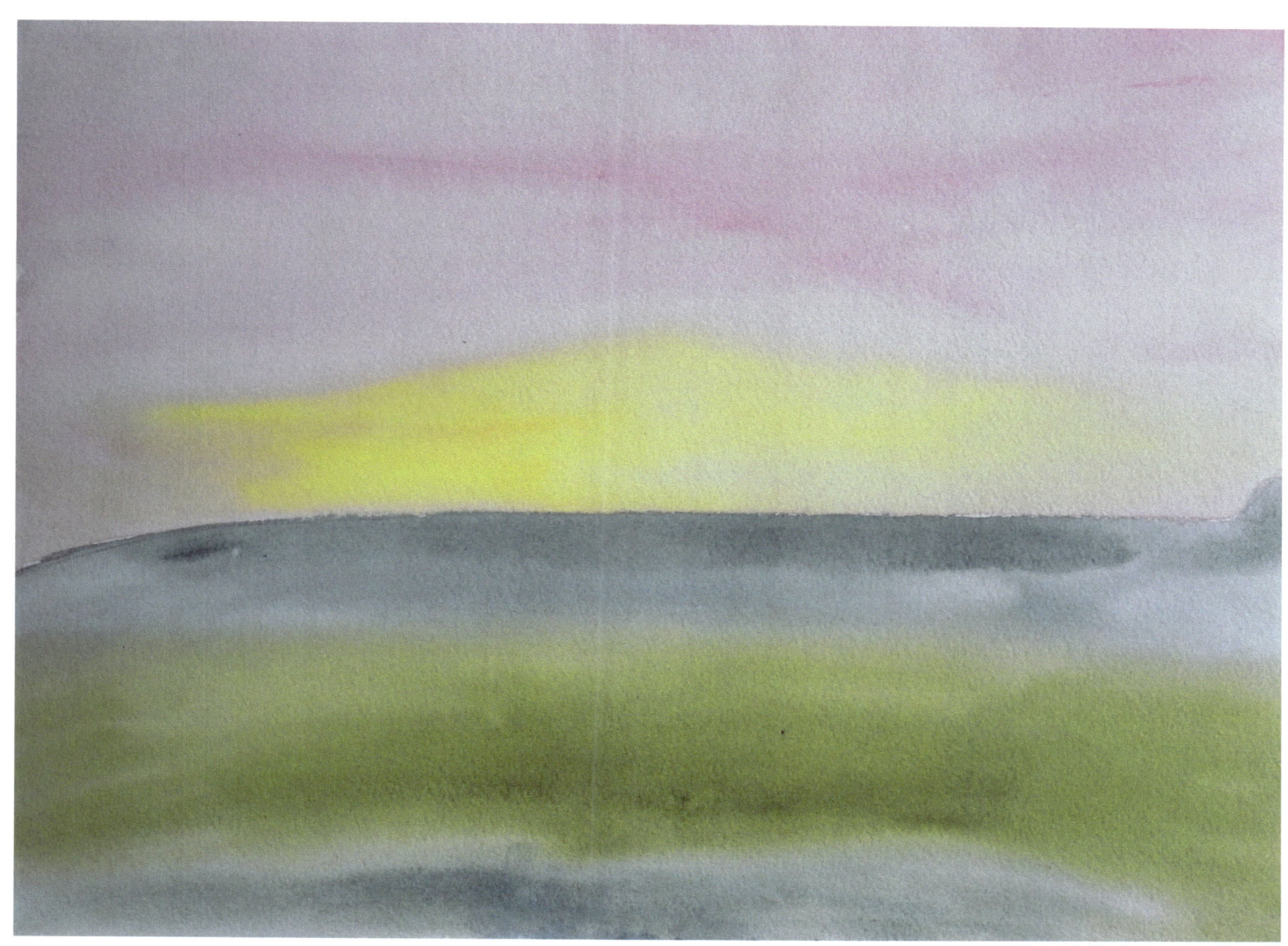

Fog and Sun North Haven

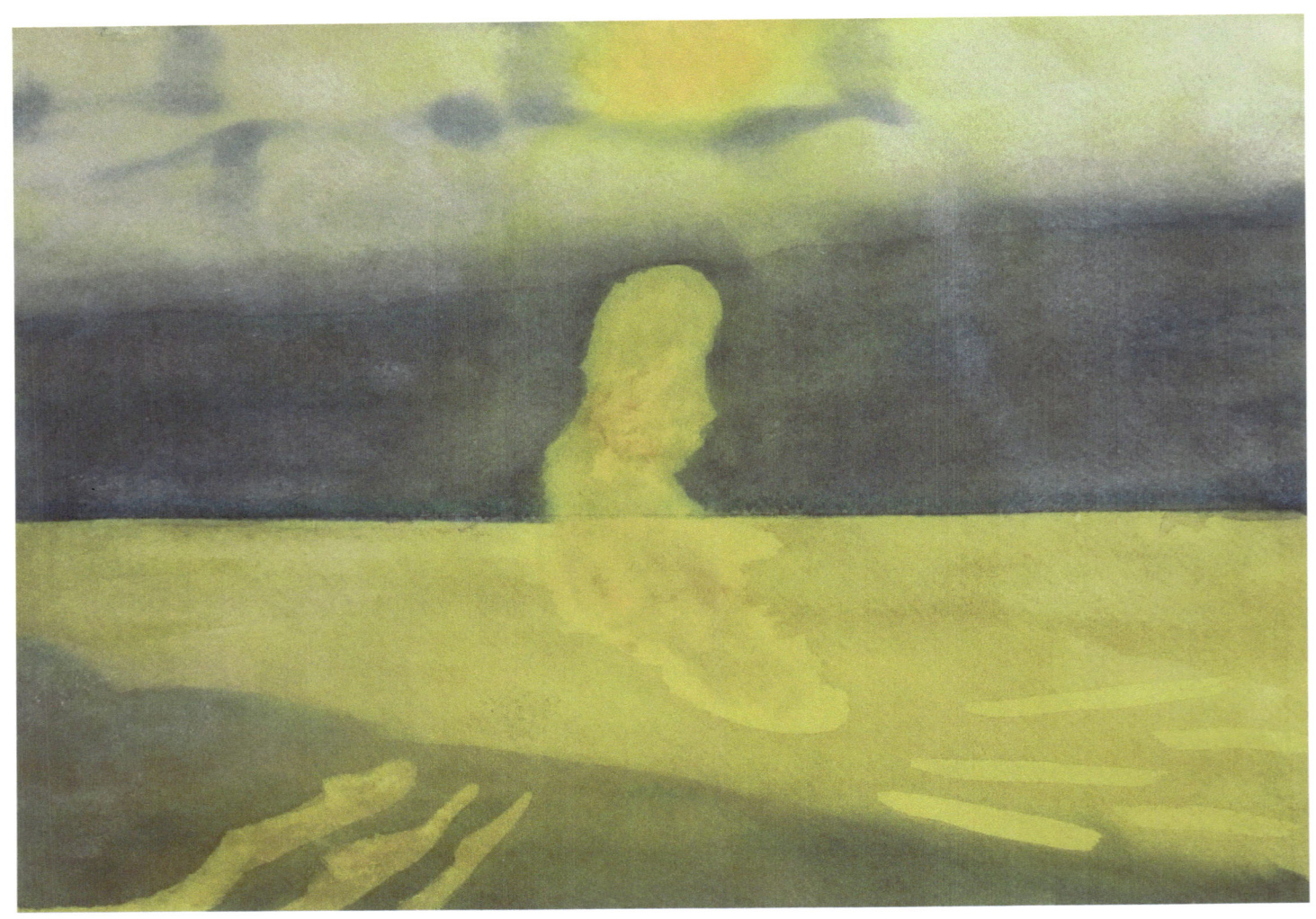

Sun Melting into the Horizon Andaman Sea

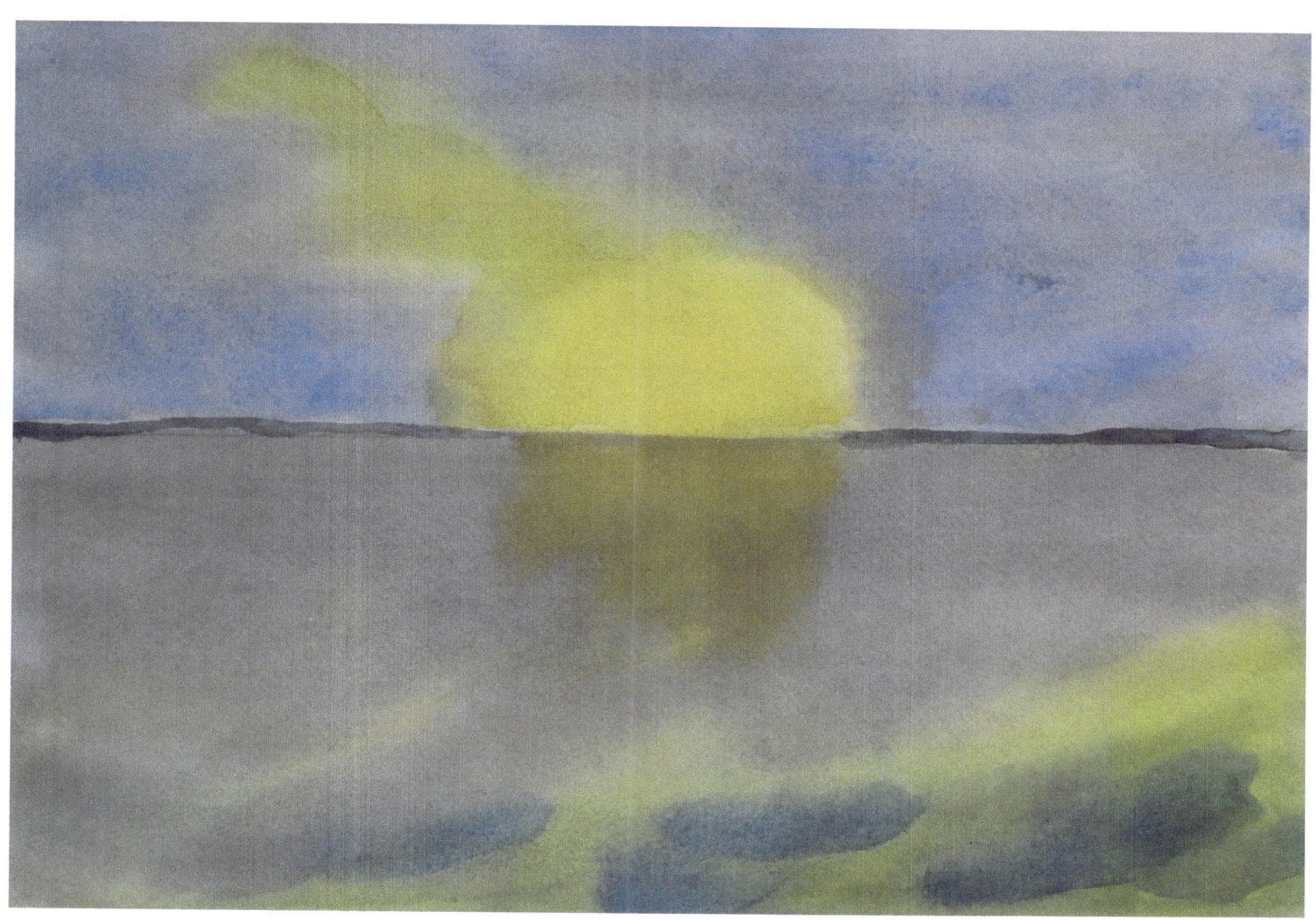

Sunset Andaman Sea

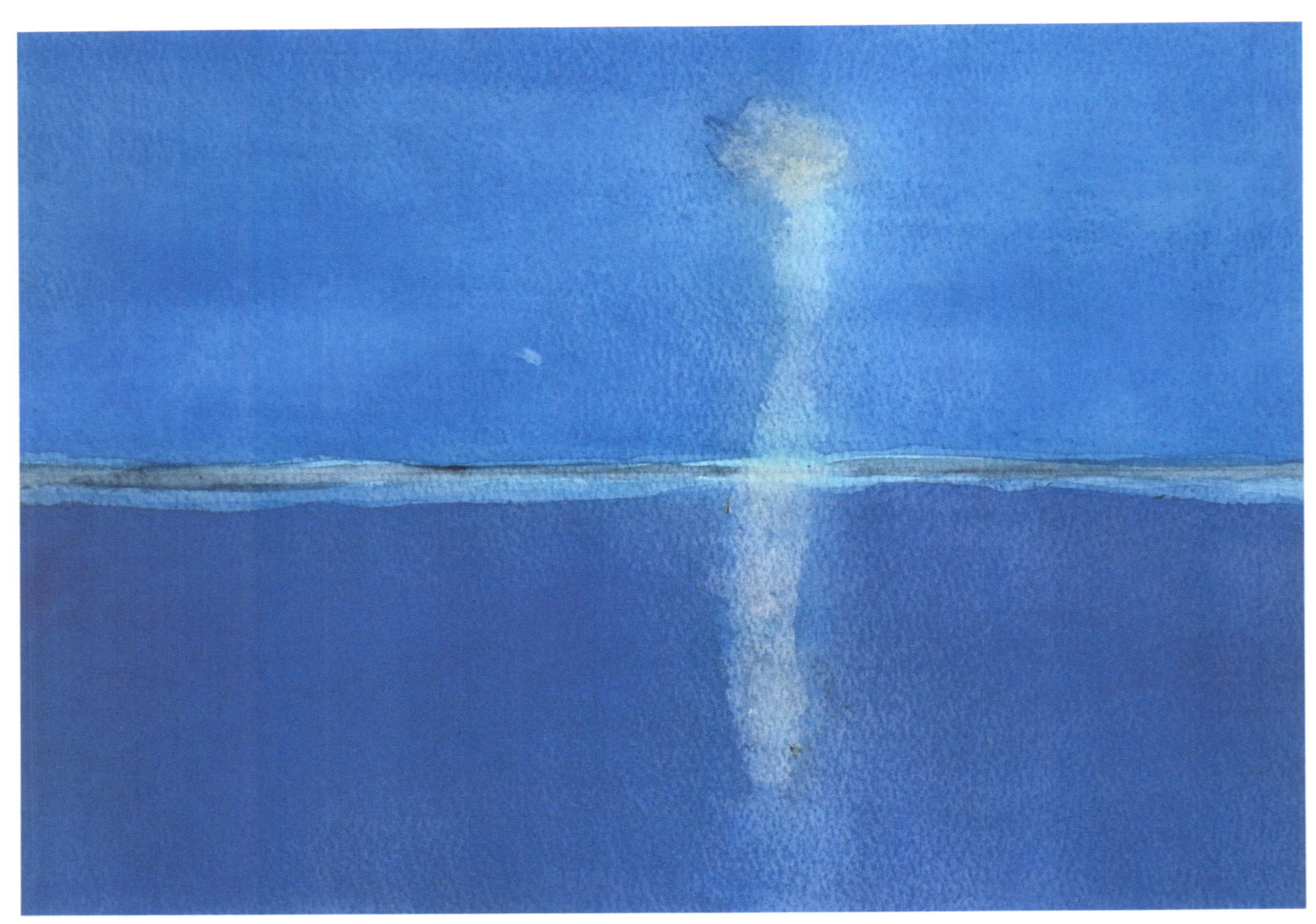

Moonlight Over Penobscot Bay

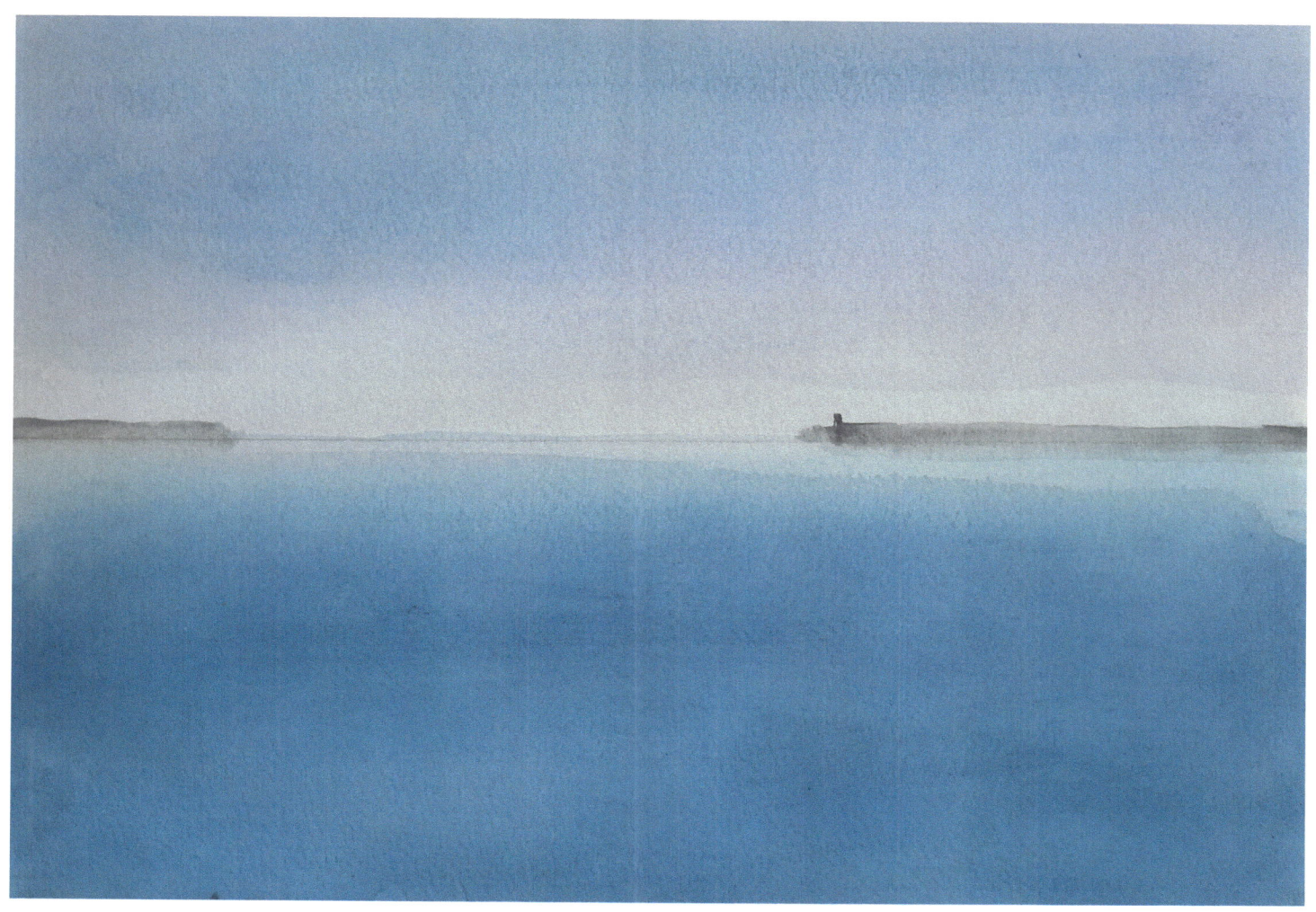

Approaching Rockland Penobscot Bay

Smokey Sou'wester Off Vinalhaven

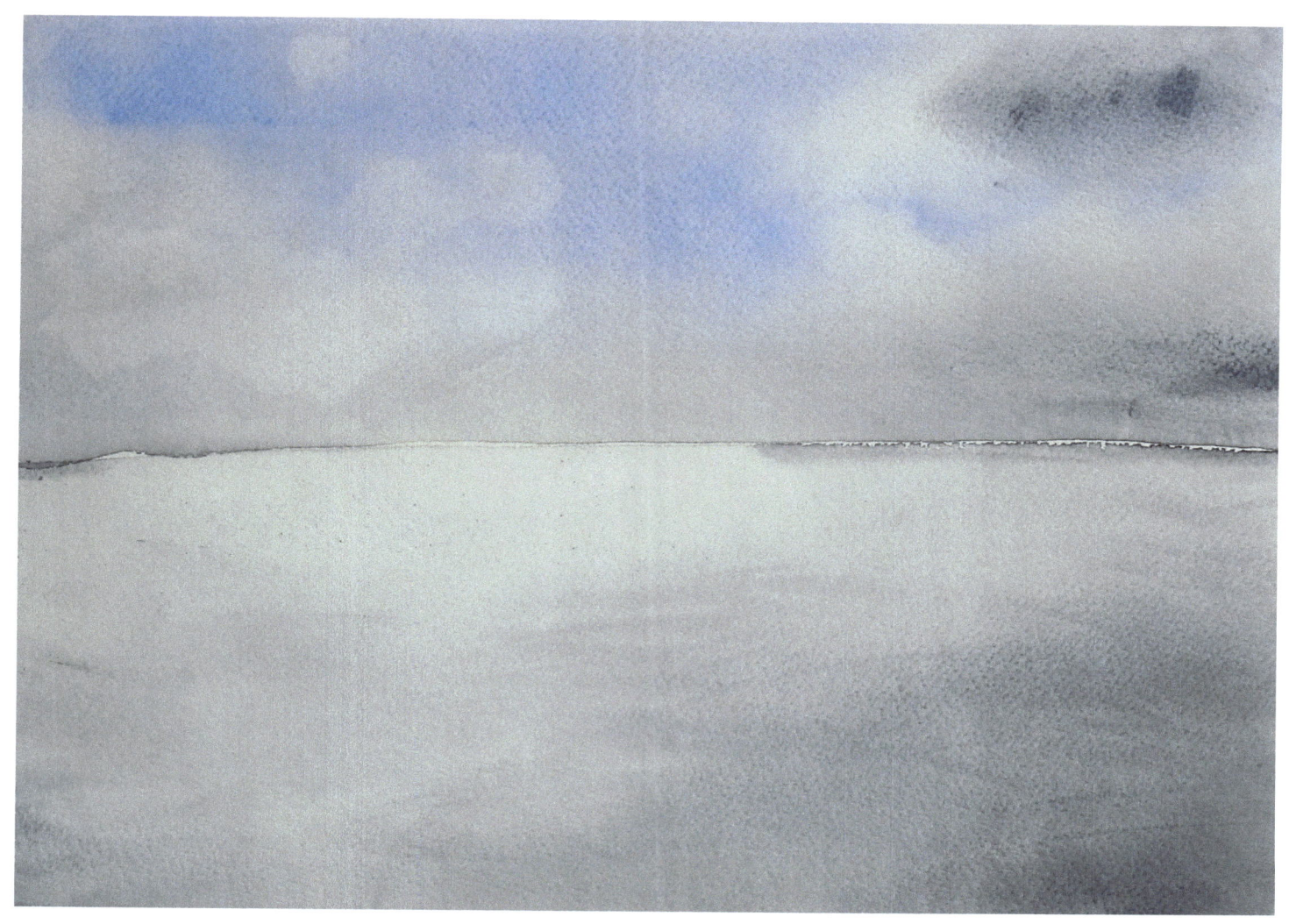

Summer Fog Coming In Penobscot Bay

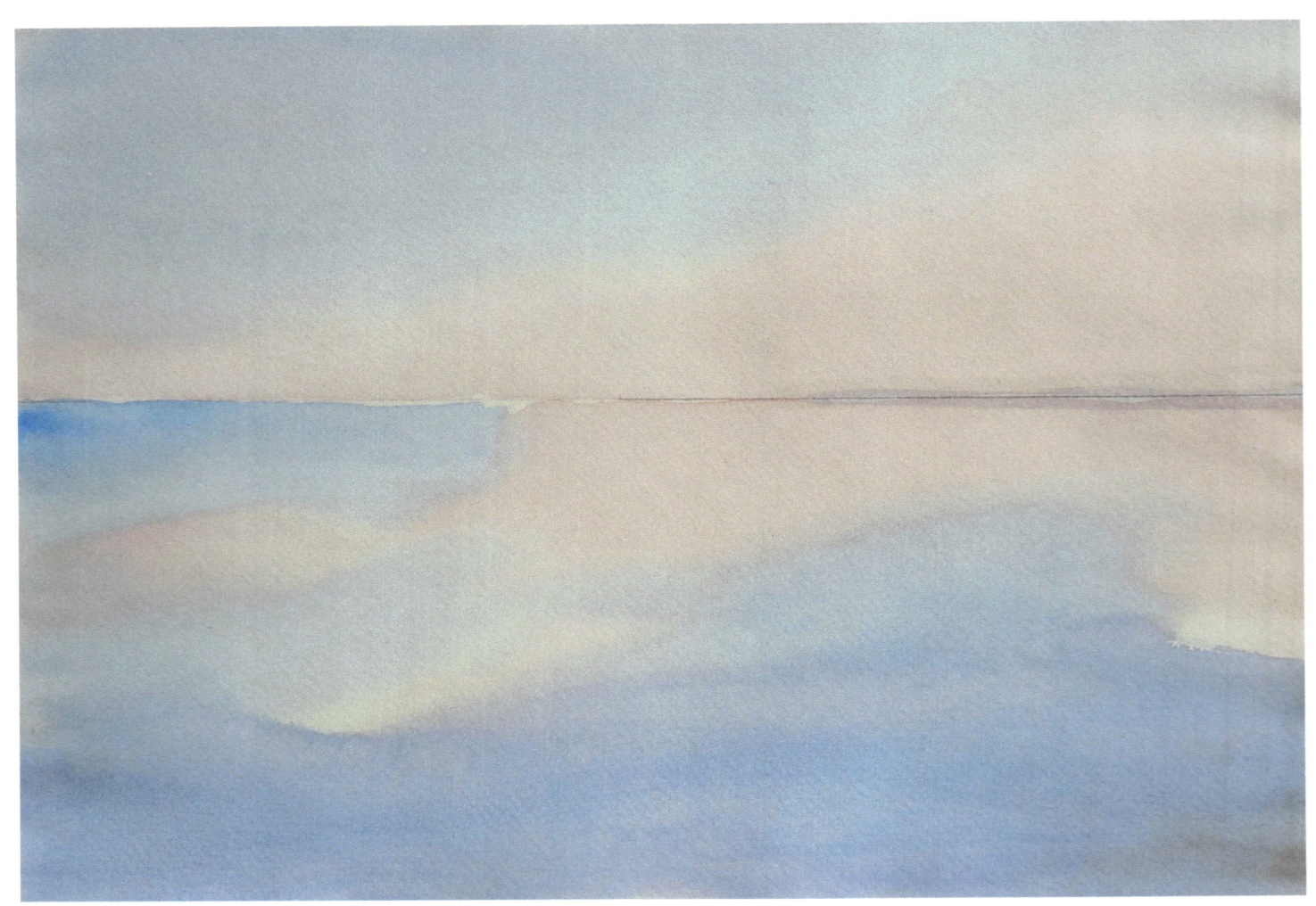

Soft Sunny Day Penobscot Bay

Grey Day Penobscot Bay

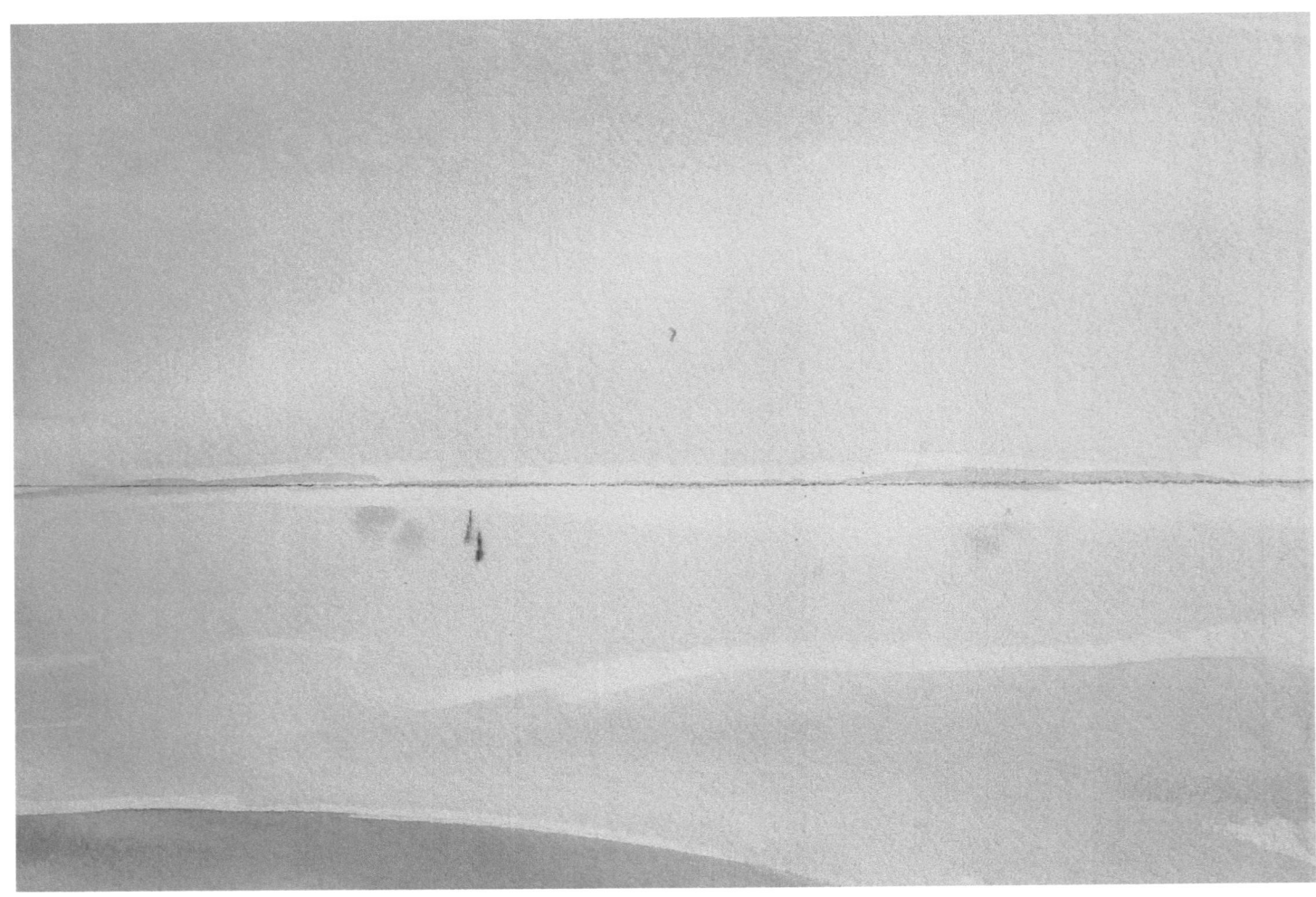

Misty Fog Isleboro

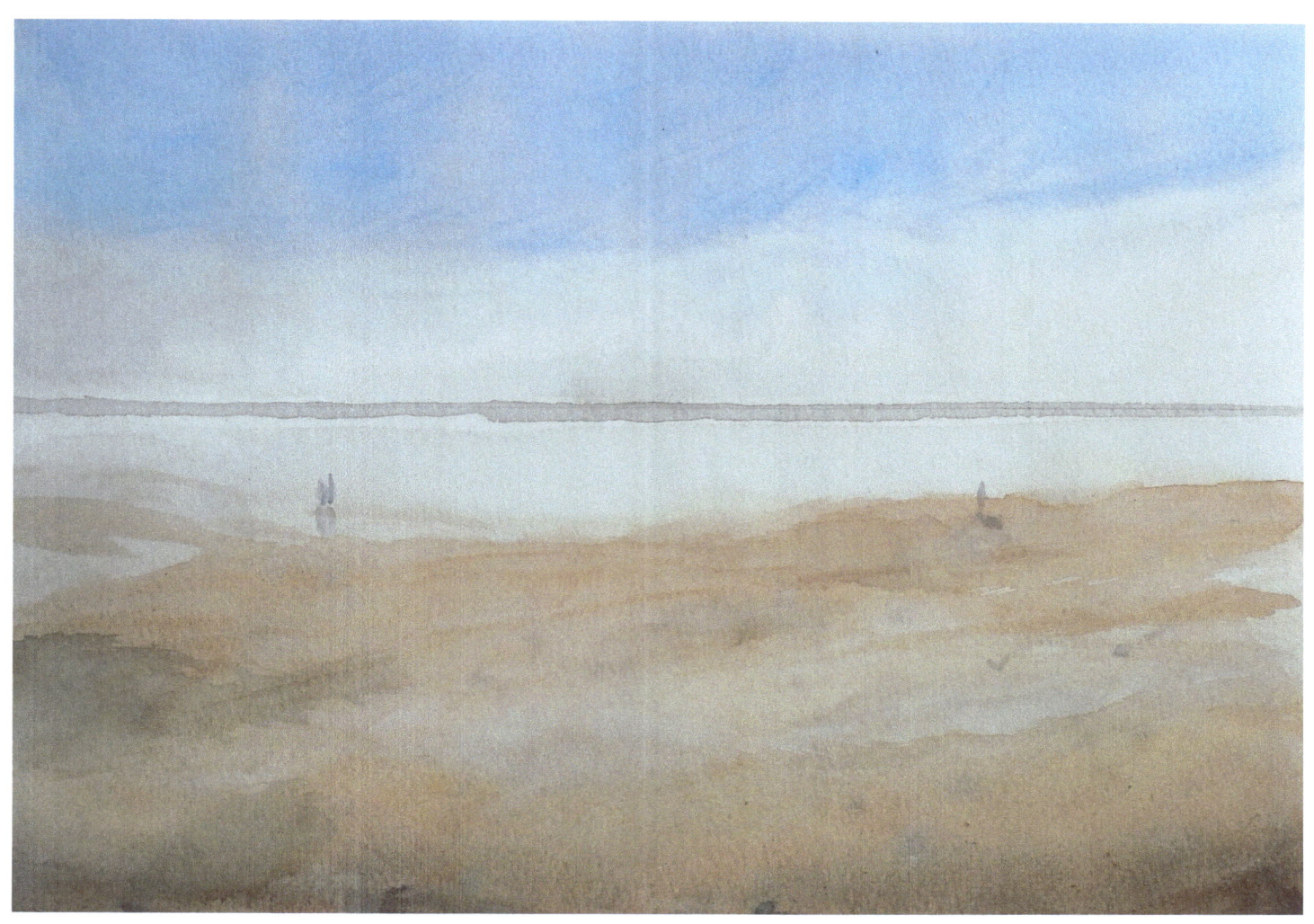

Low Tide

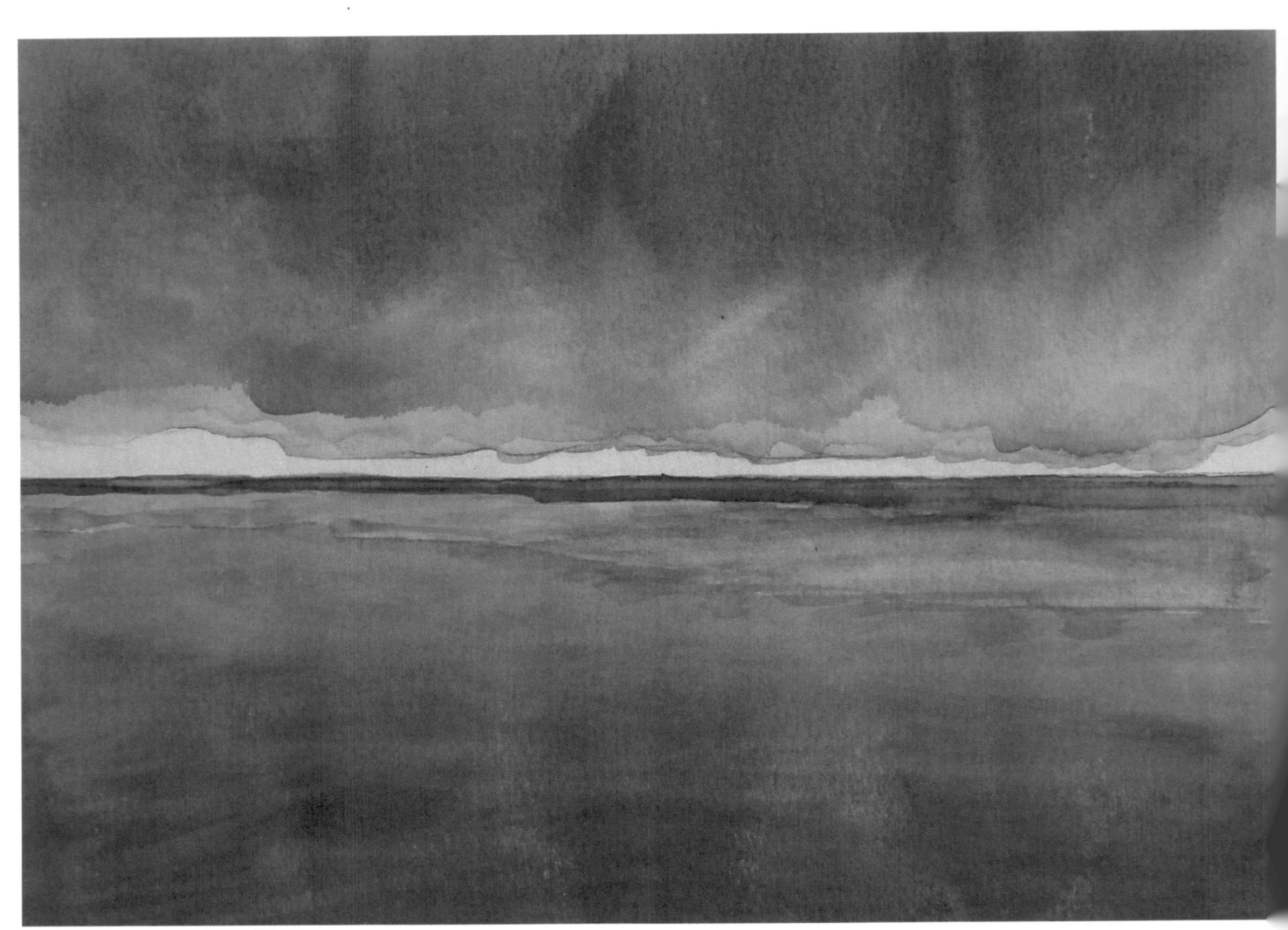

Summer Squall Casco Bay

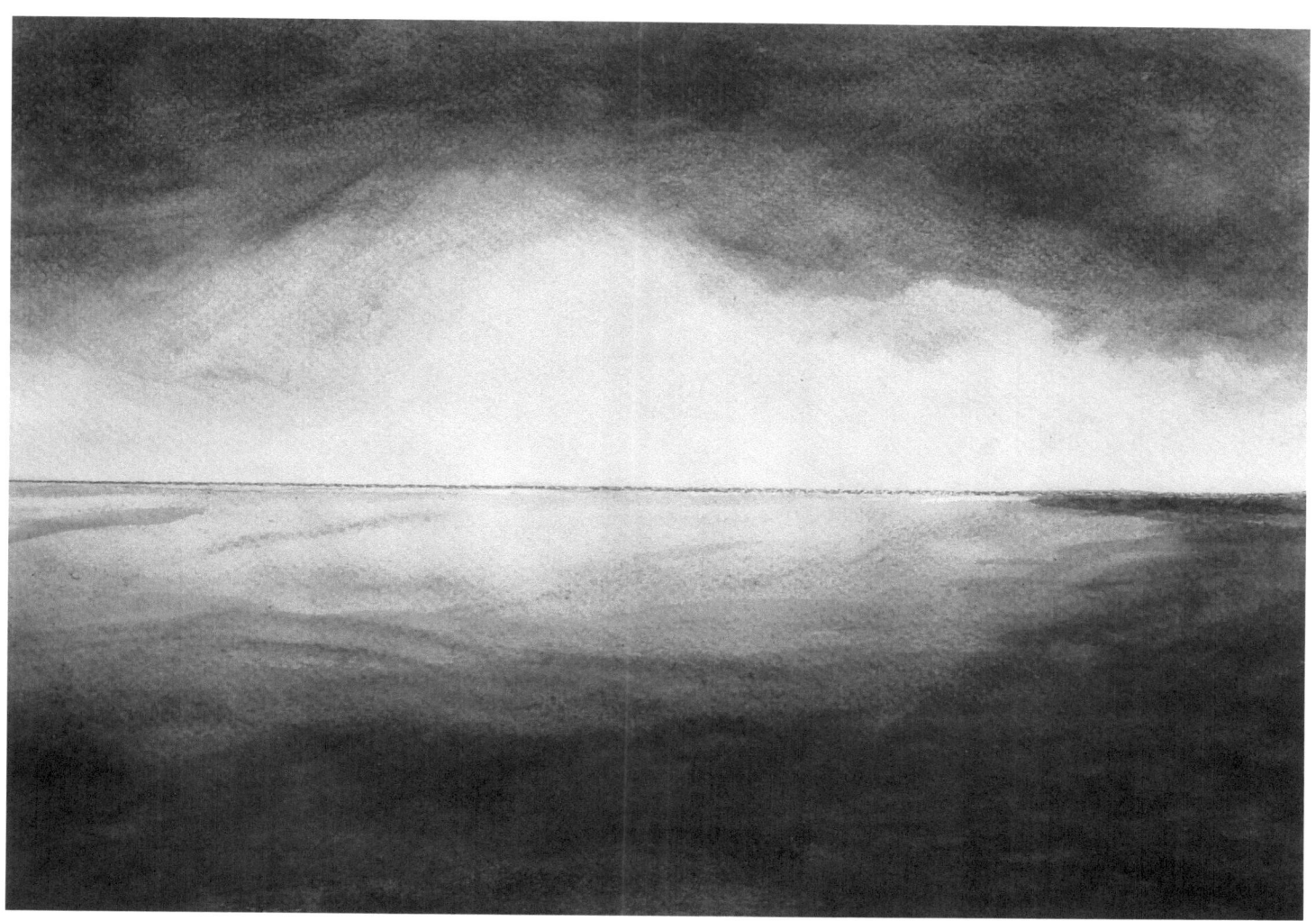

Stormy Day

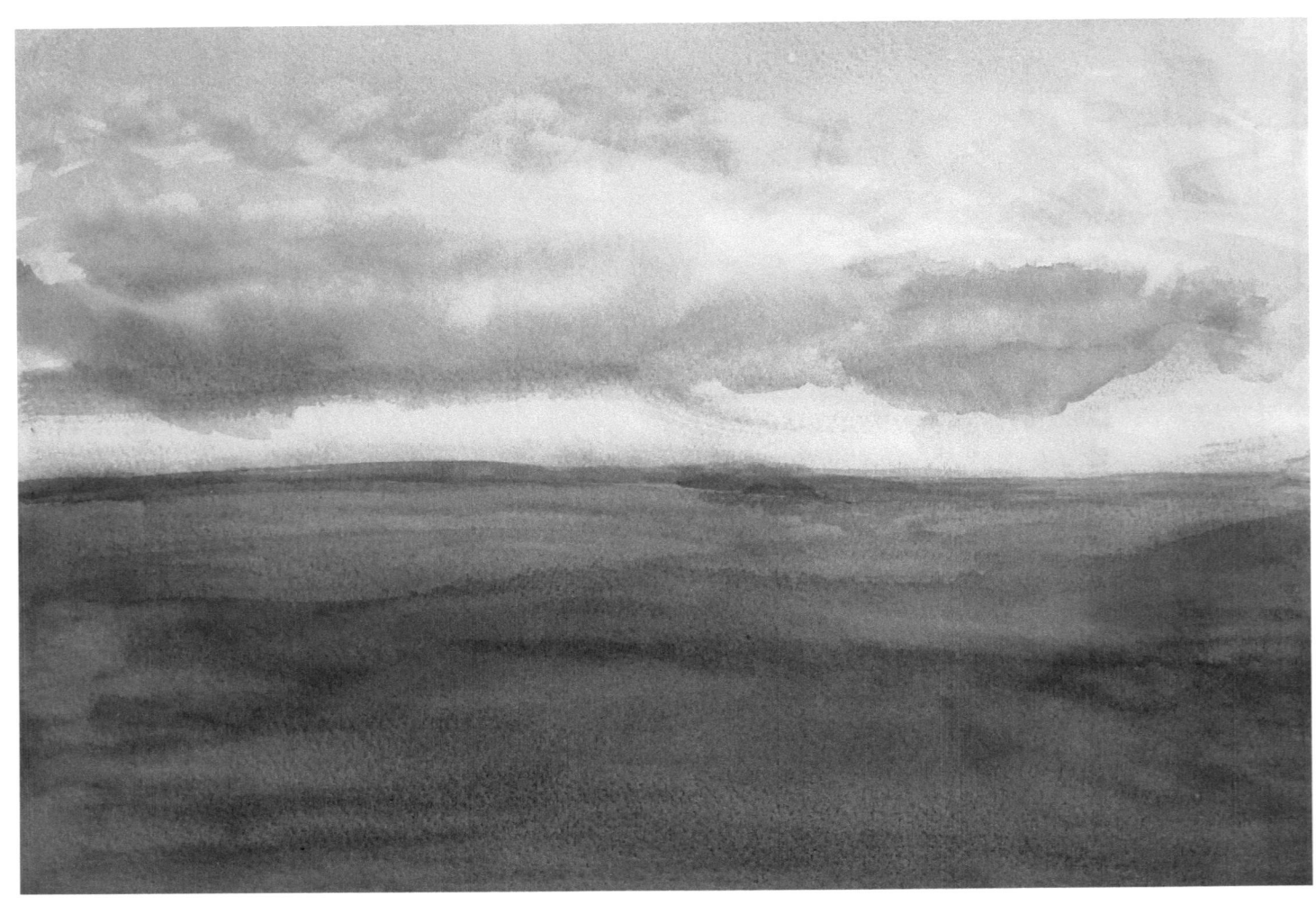

Stormy Sea Penobscot Bay

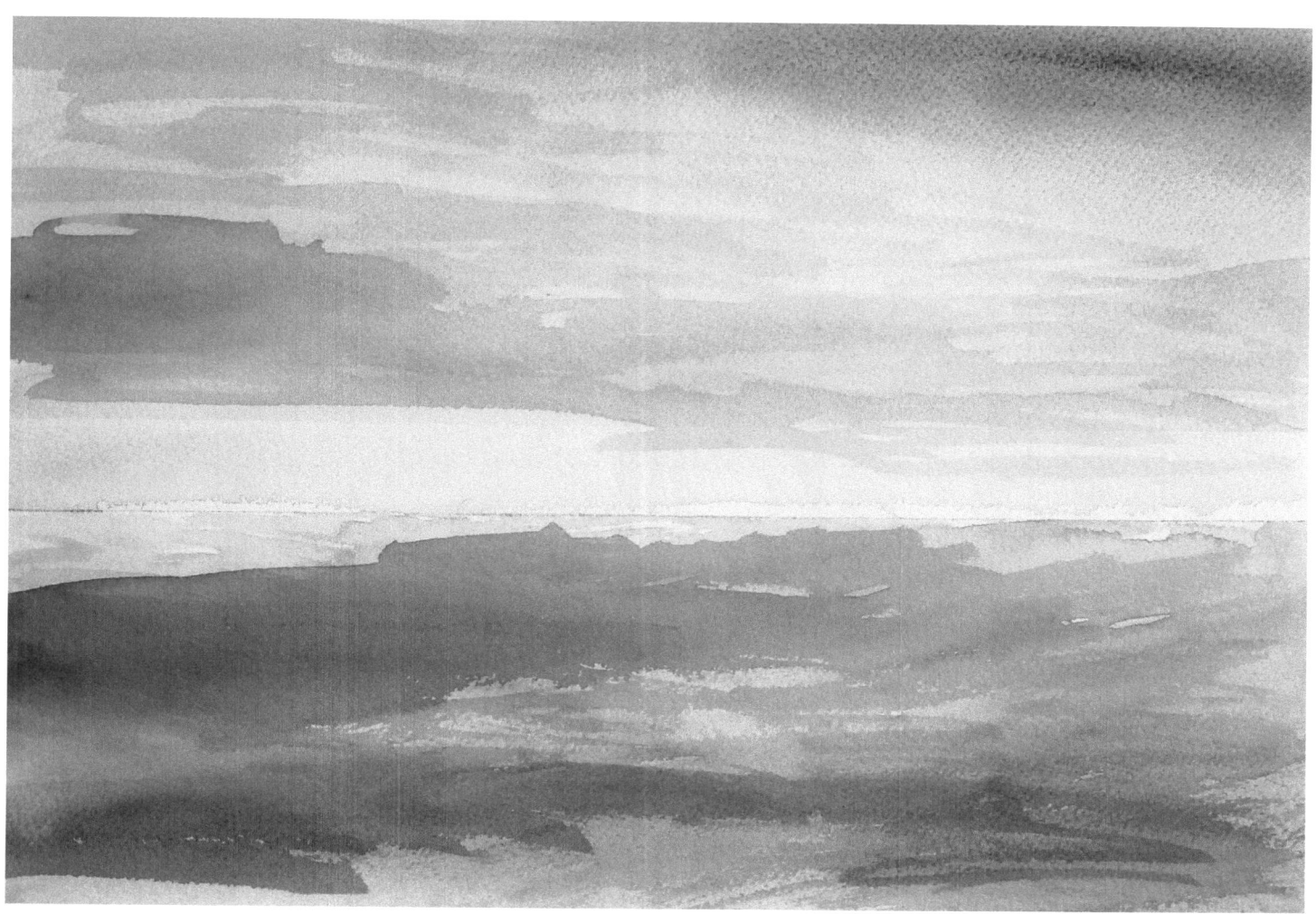

Foggy Day

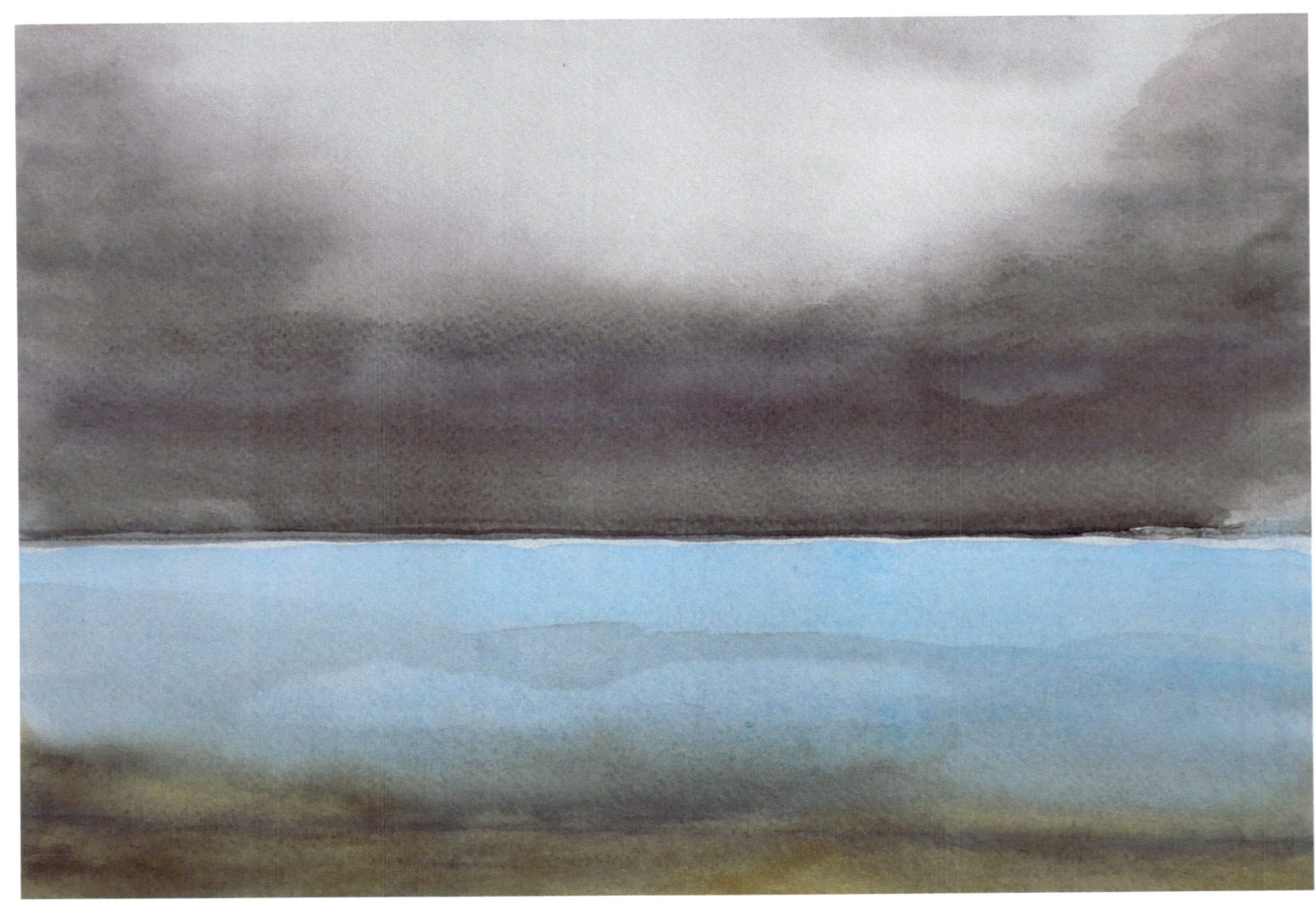

Tropical Squall Andaman Sea

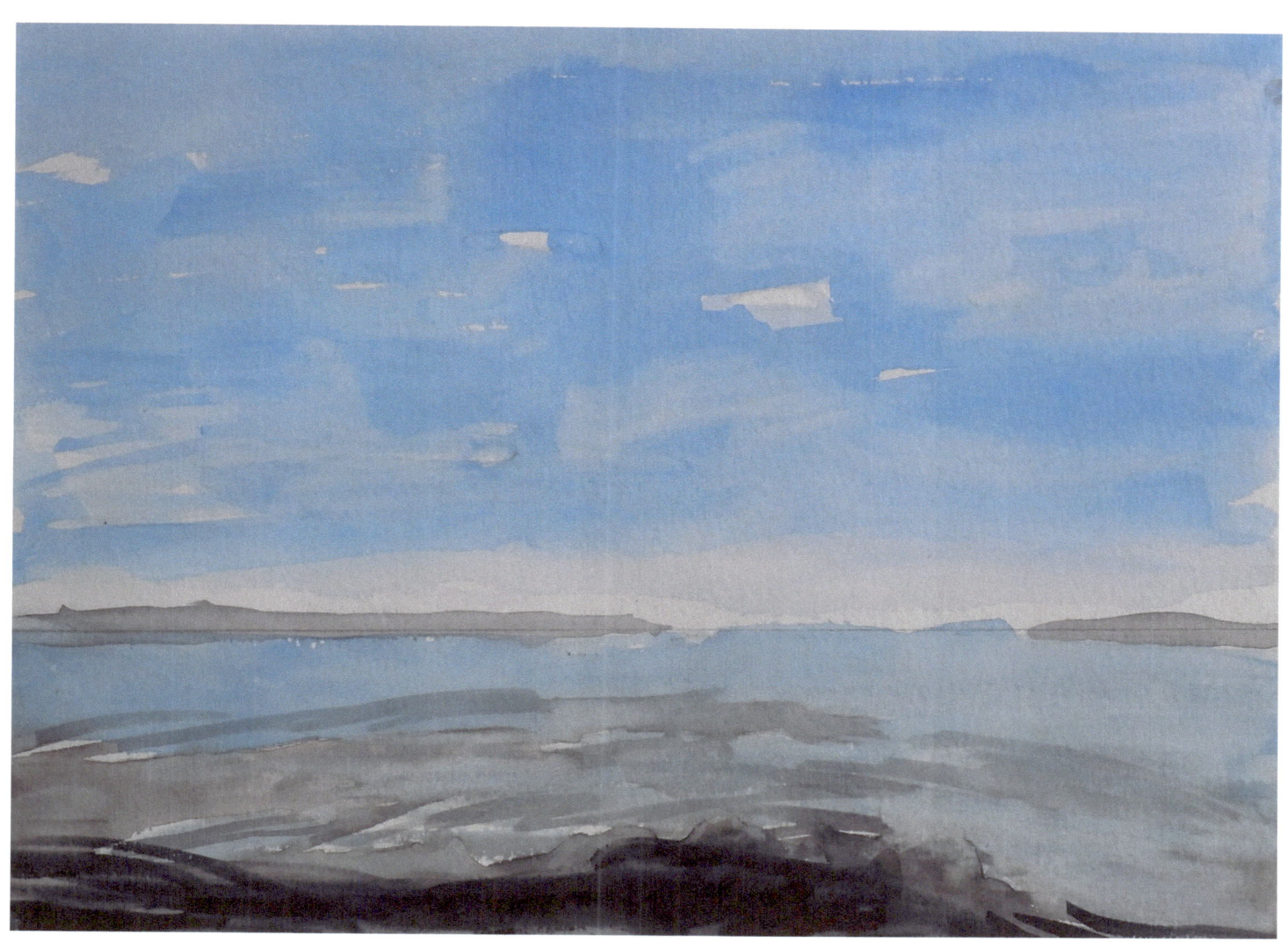

Summer Day Upper Penobscot Bay

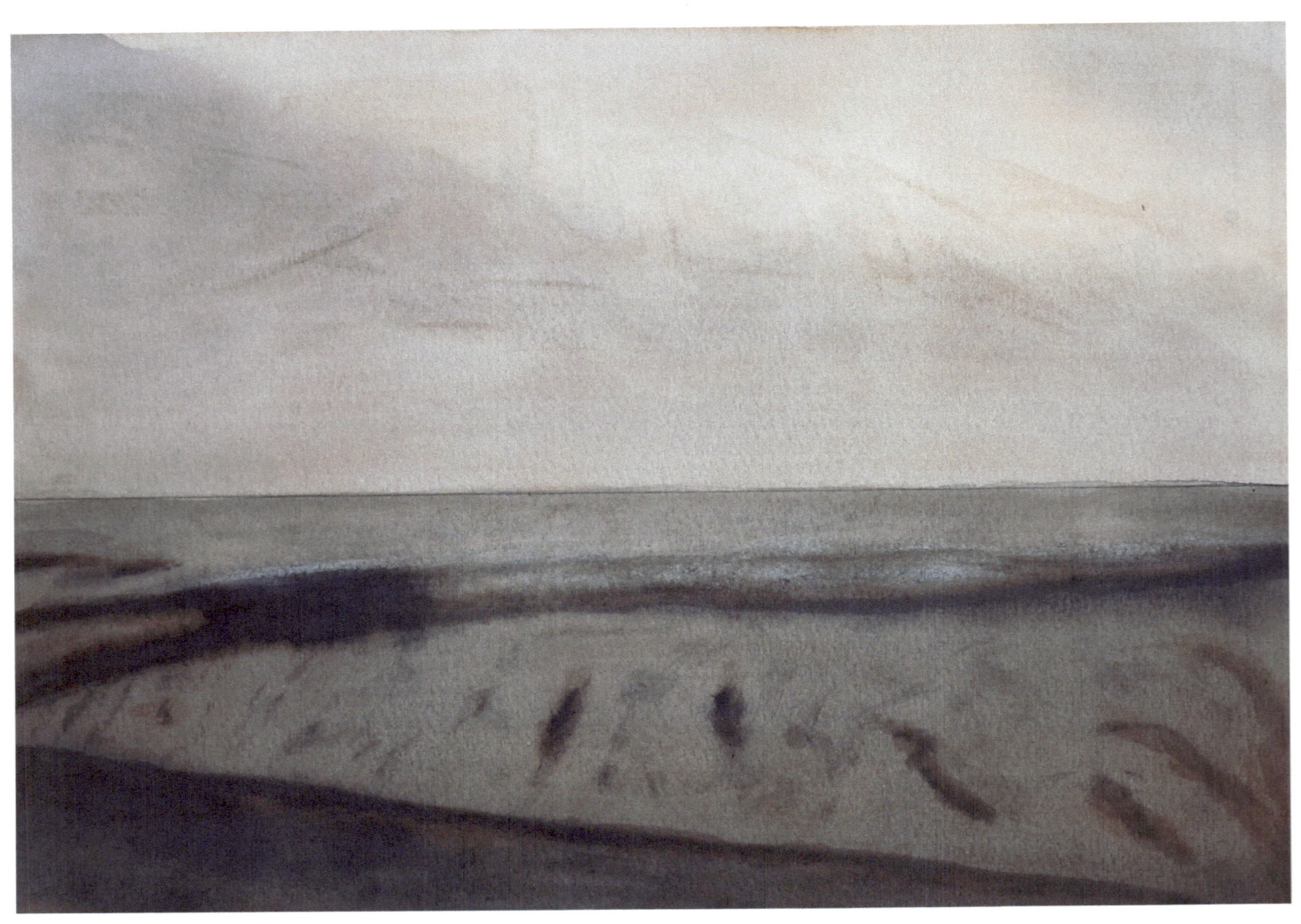

Mud Flats Tenants Harbor

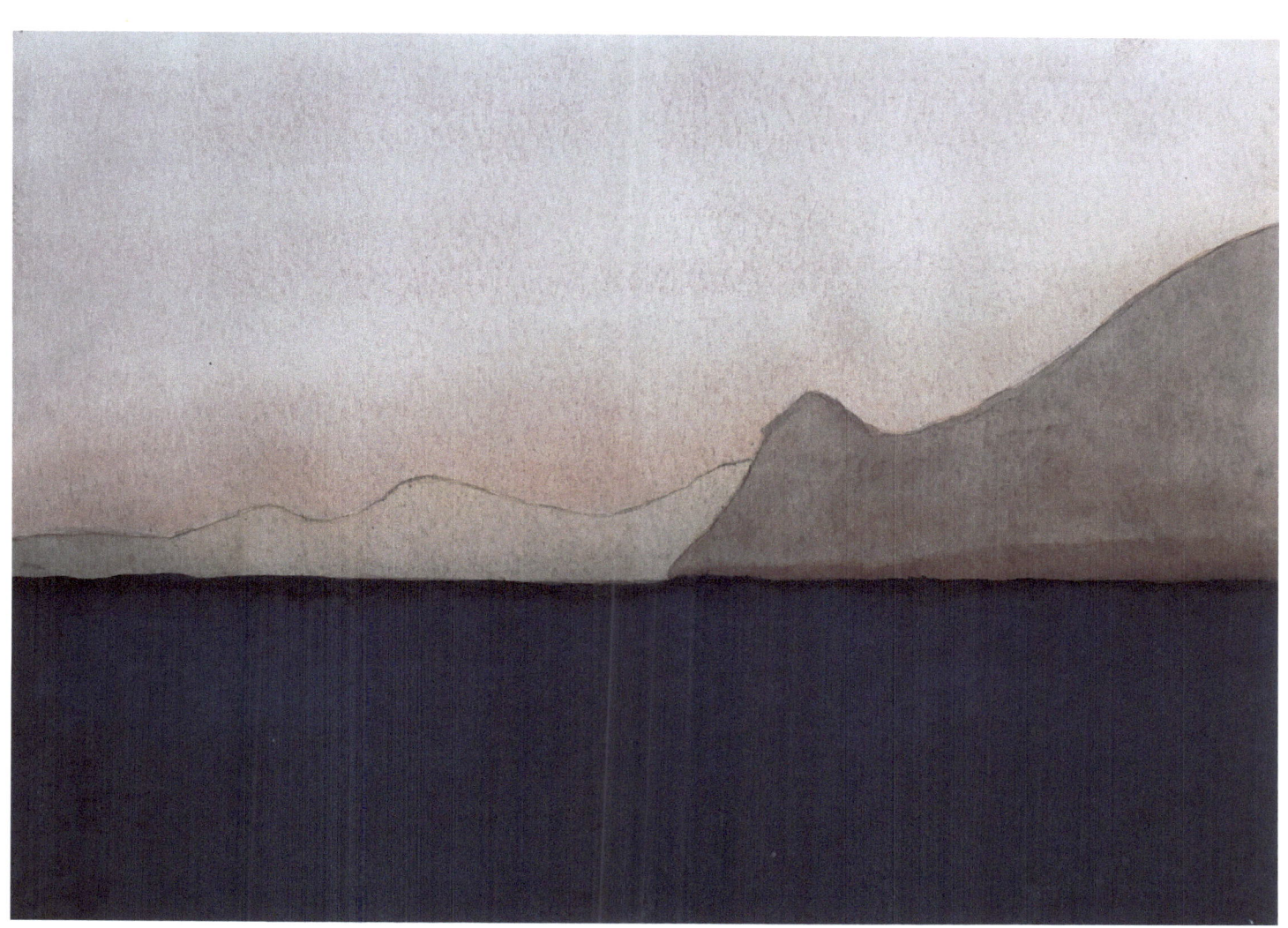

Baja Coast Mexico

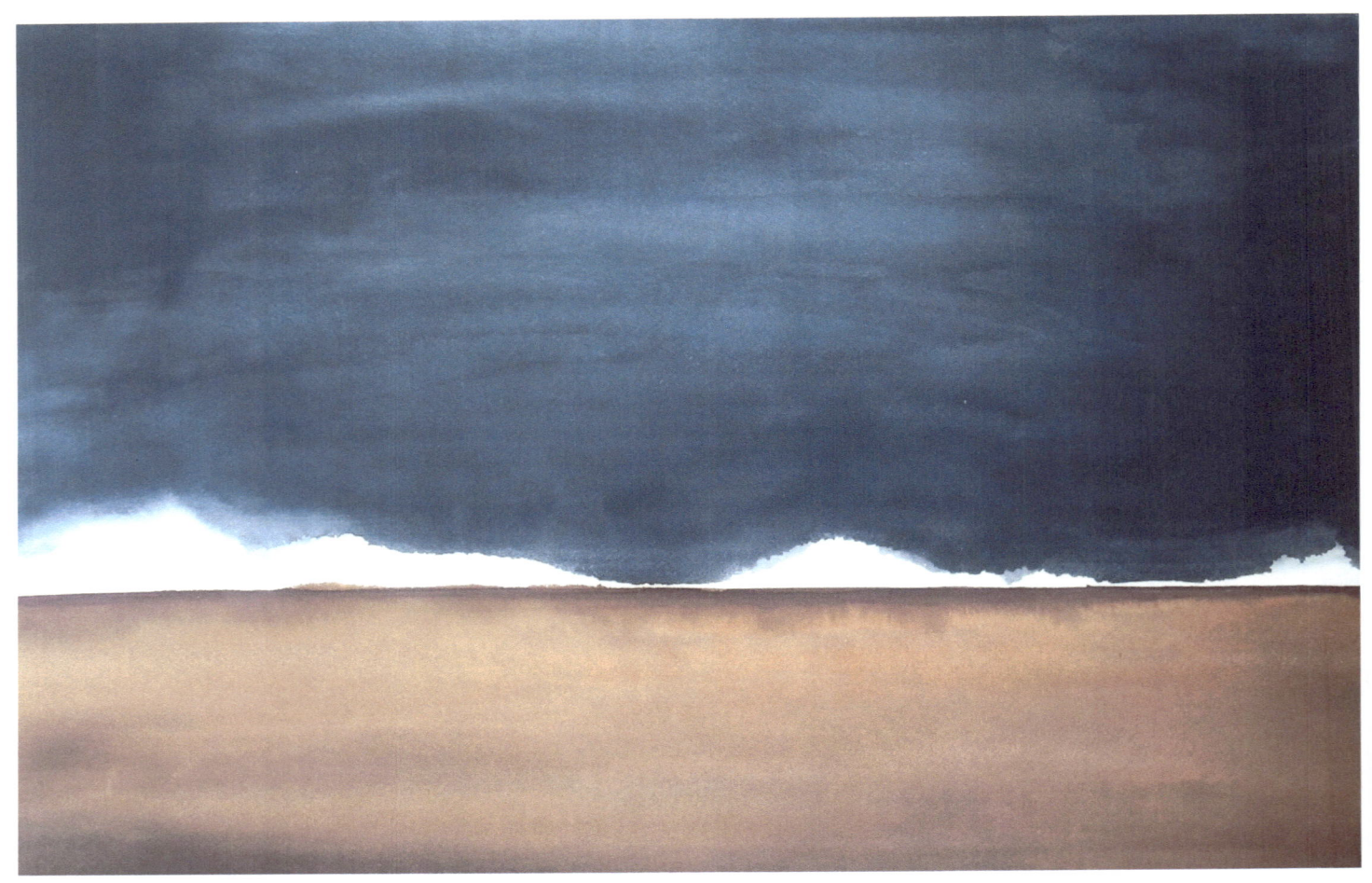

Desert Thunder Storm

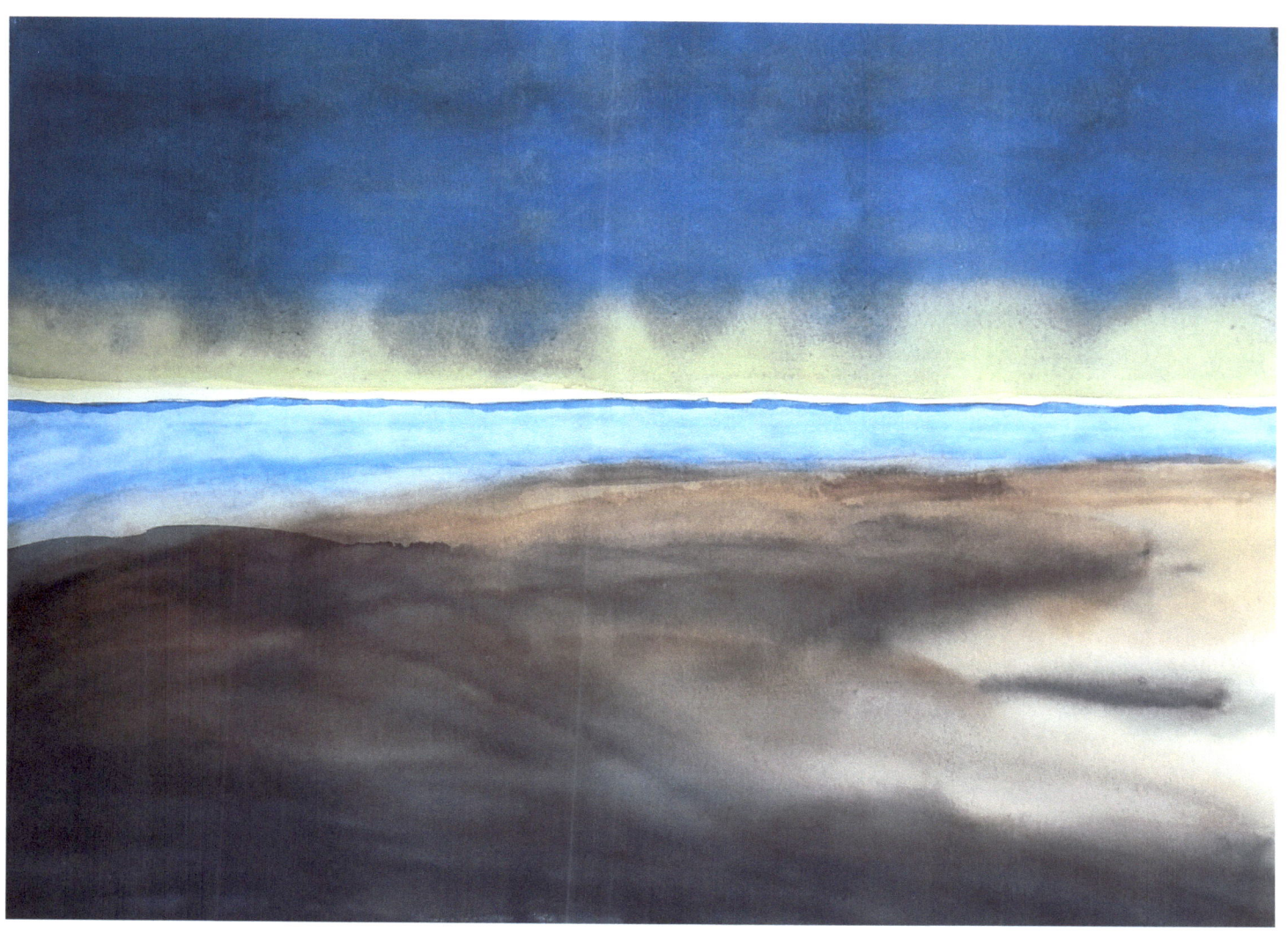

Summer Rain Squall Vinalhaven

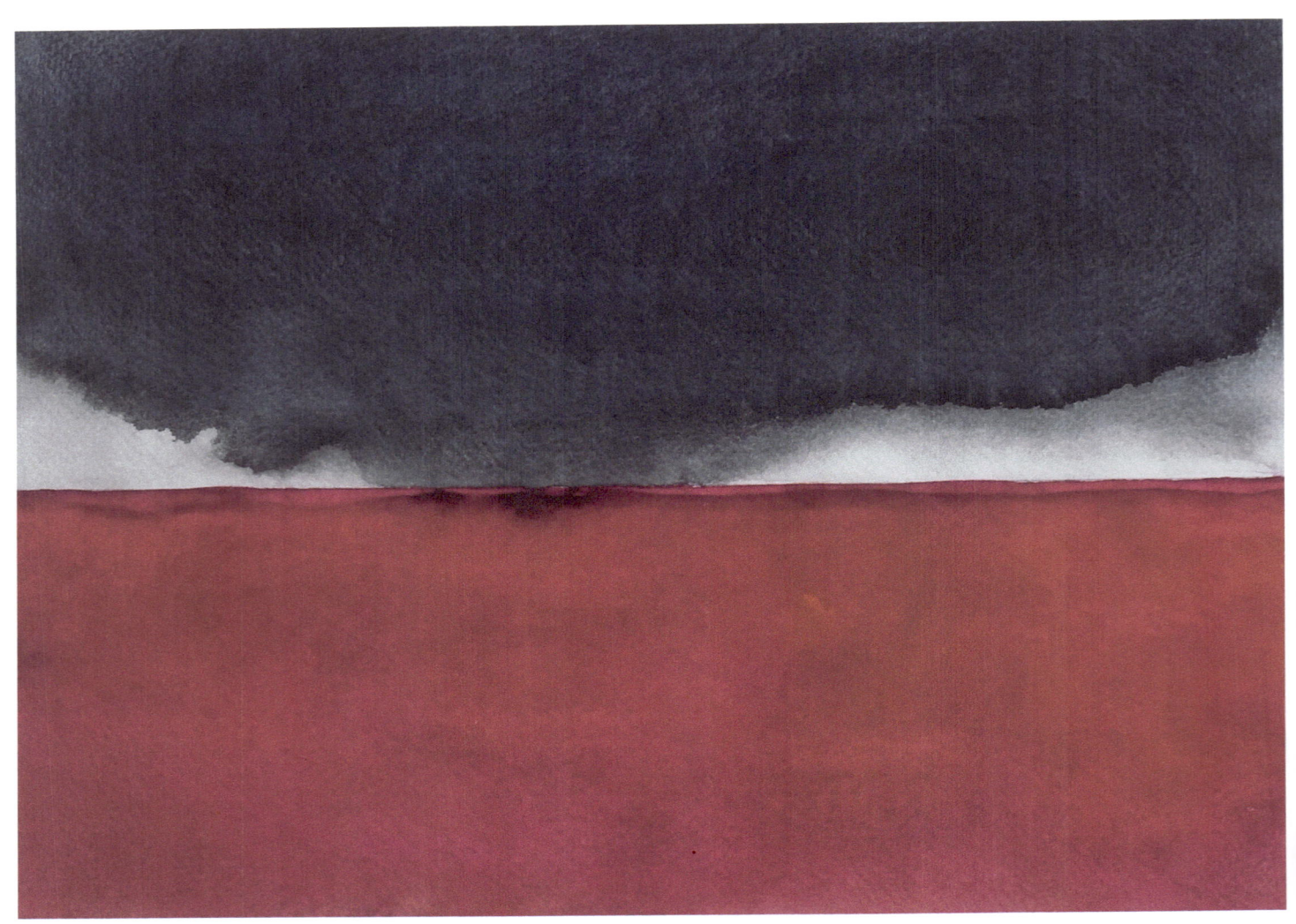

Heavy Squall Over Red Landscape

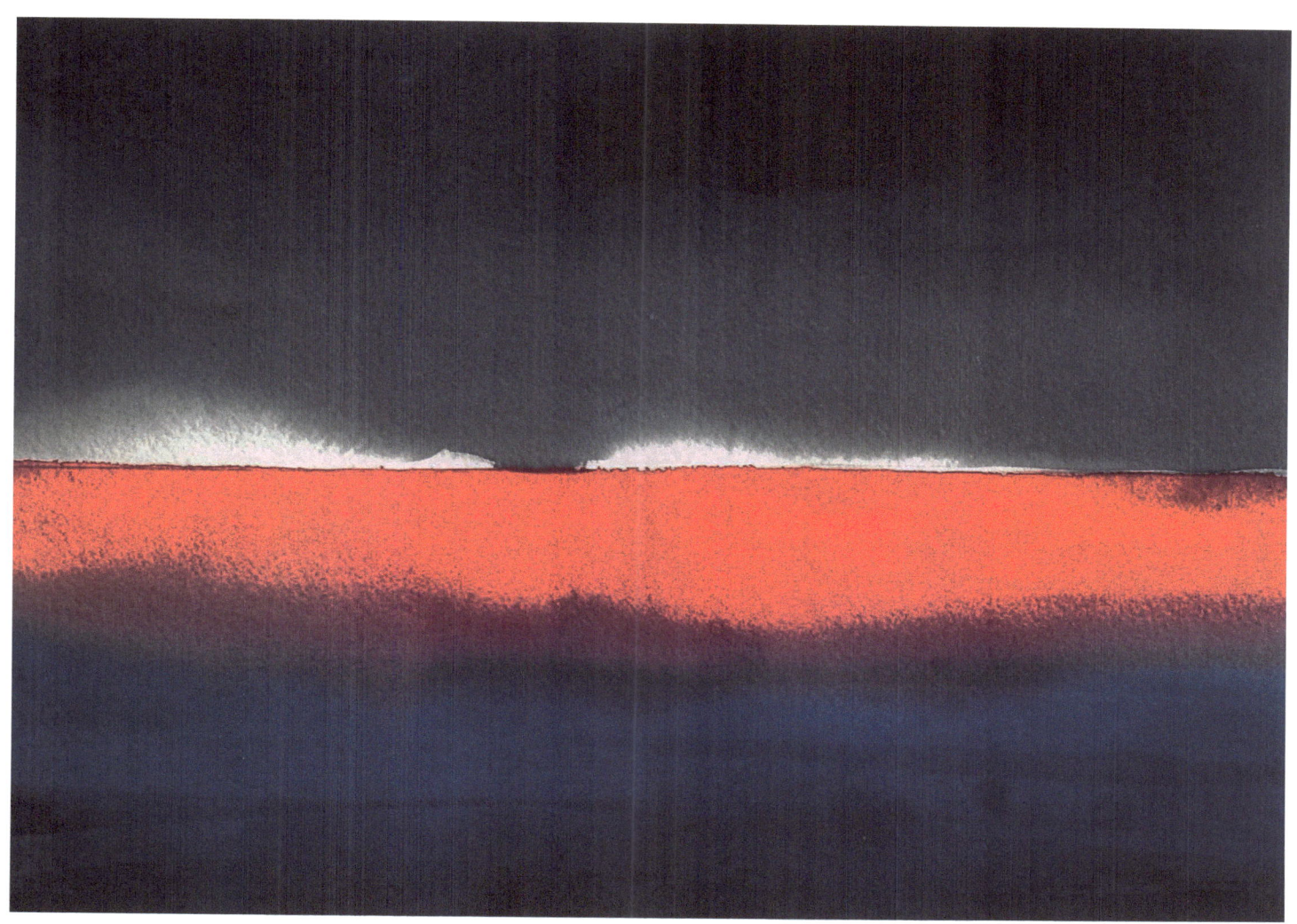

Dawn Storm

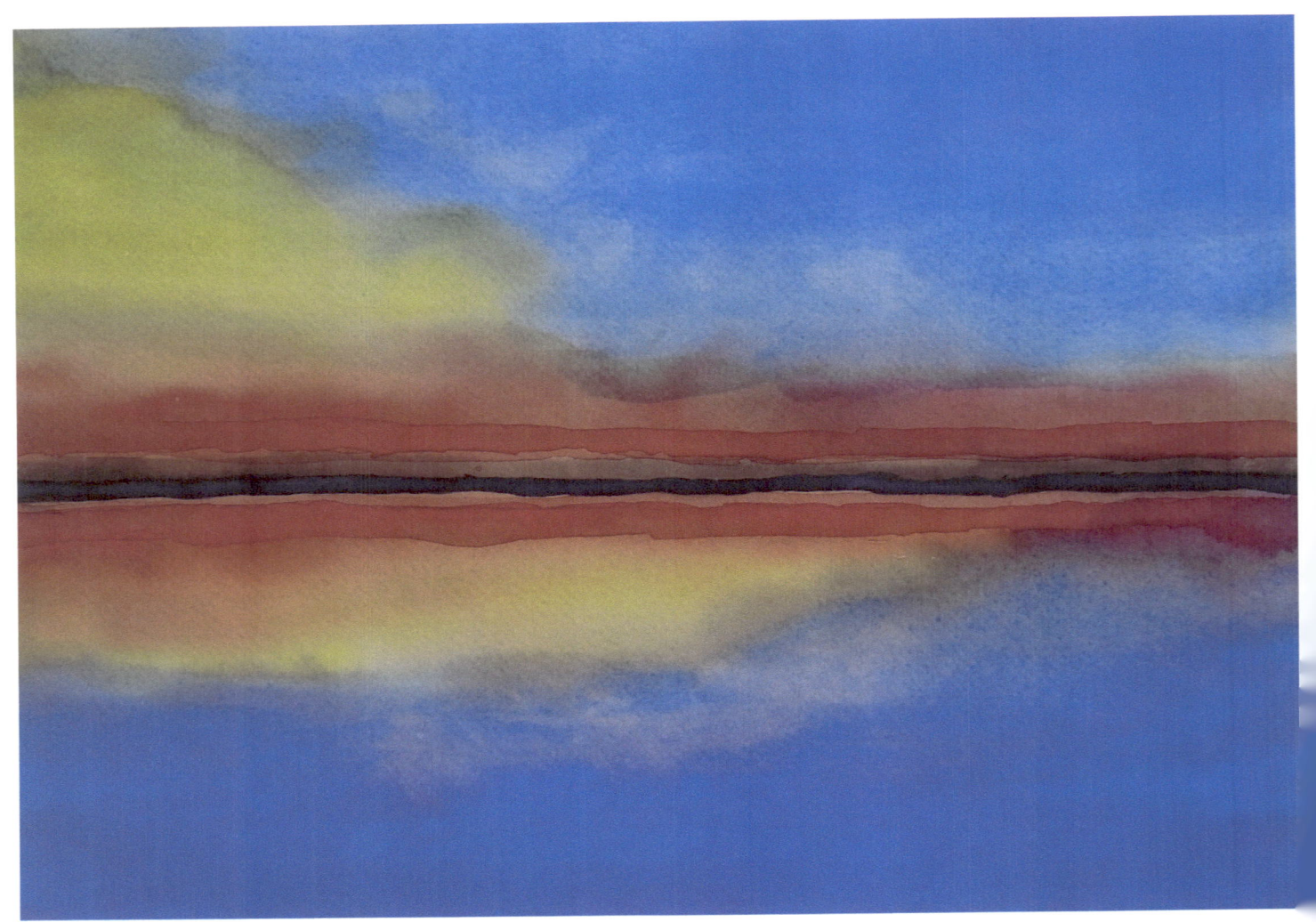

Brilliant Dawn Penobscot Bay

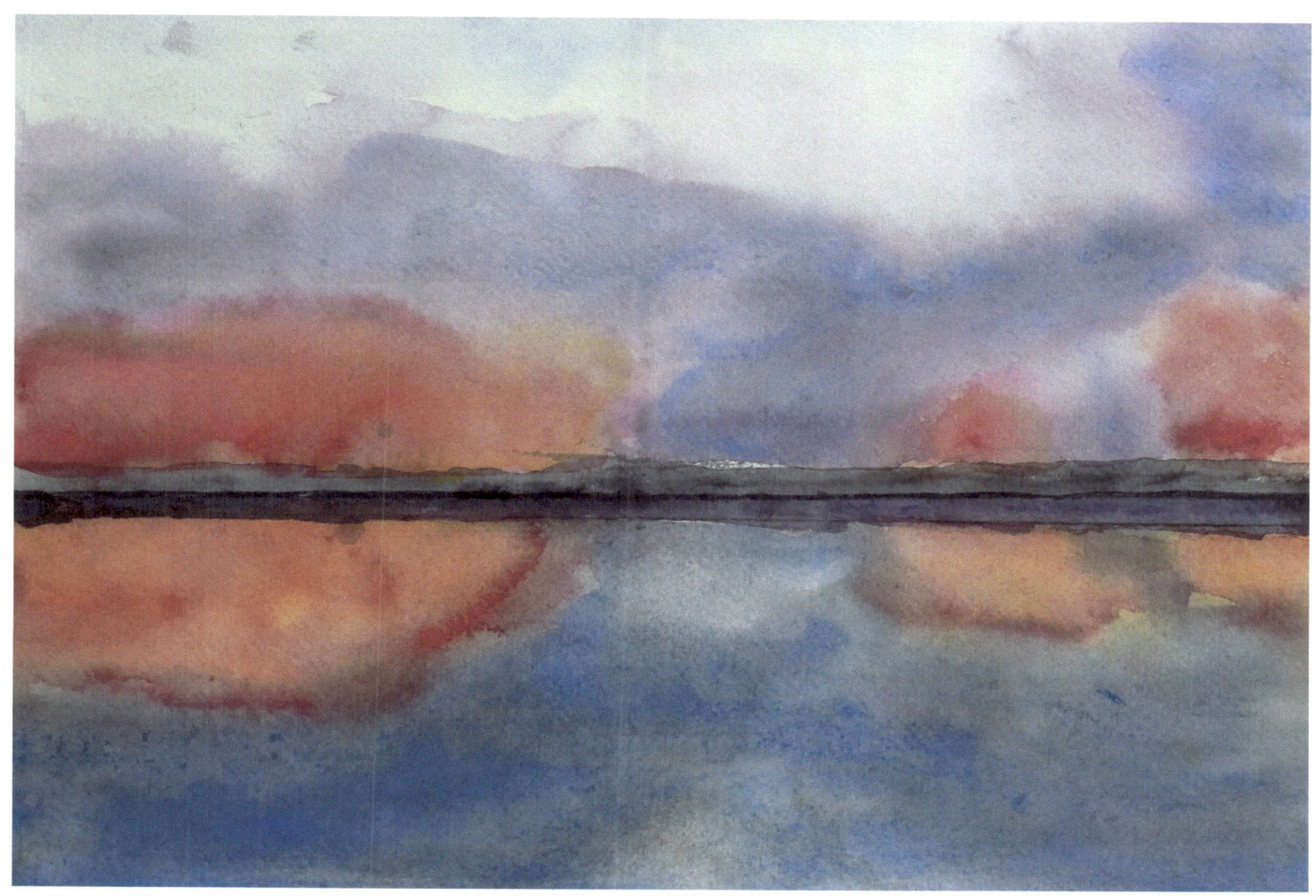

Foggy Dawn Deer Isle

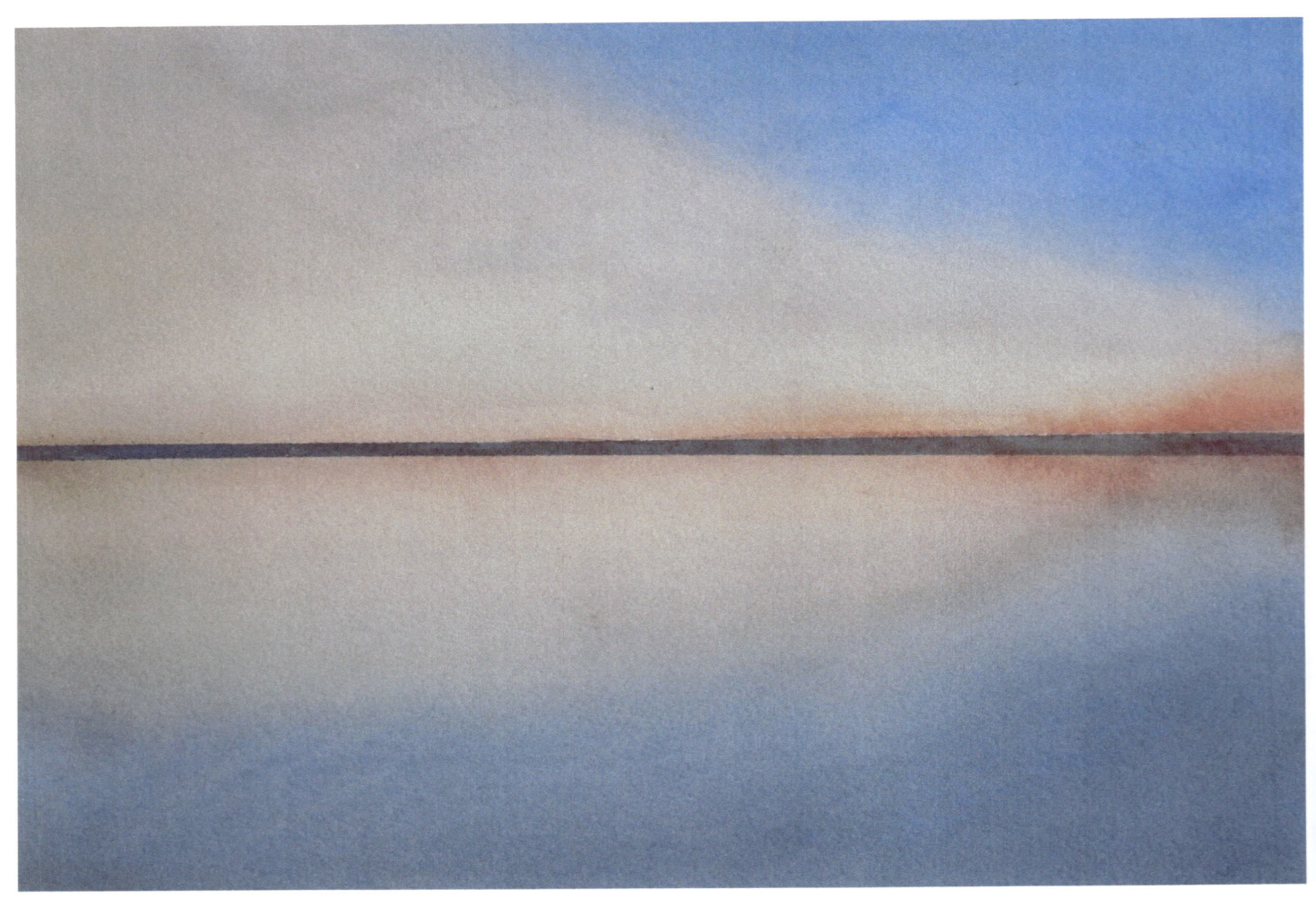

Still Dawn from Monhegan Island

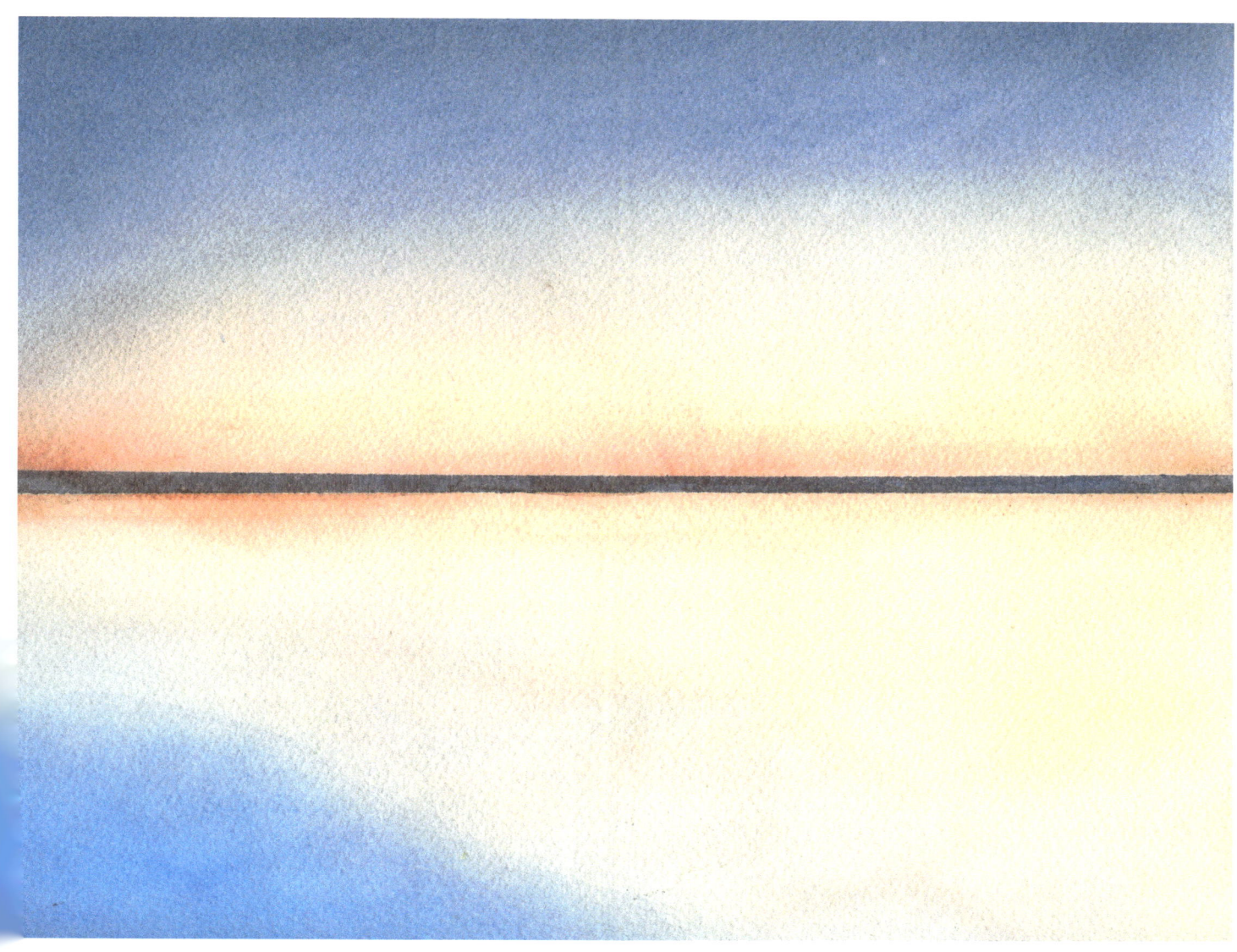

Sunrise Monhegan Island

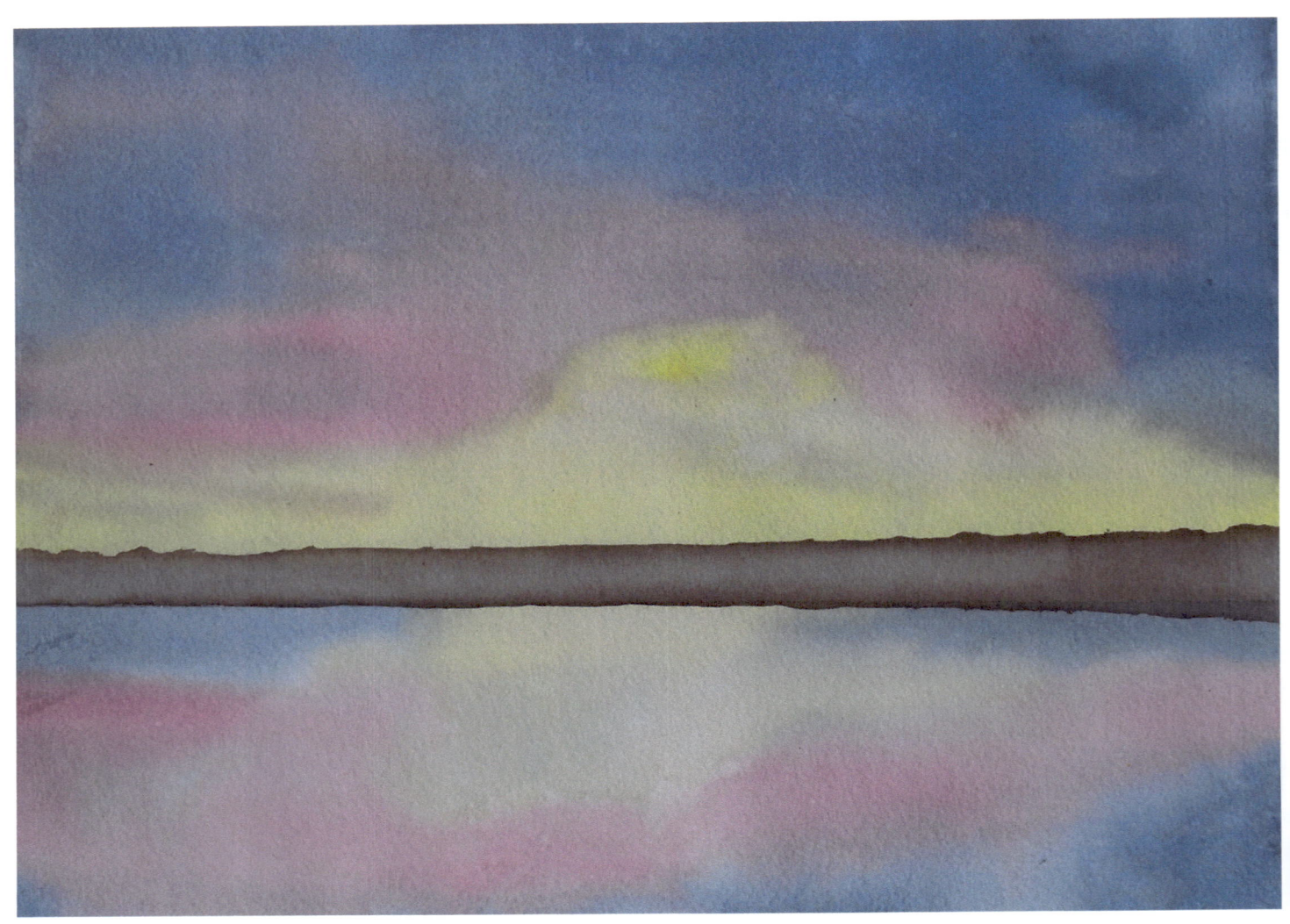

Andaman Sea Sunrise

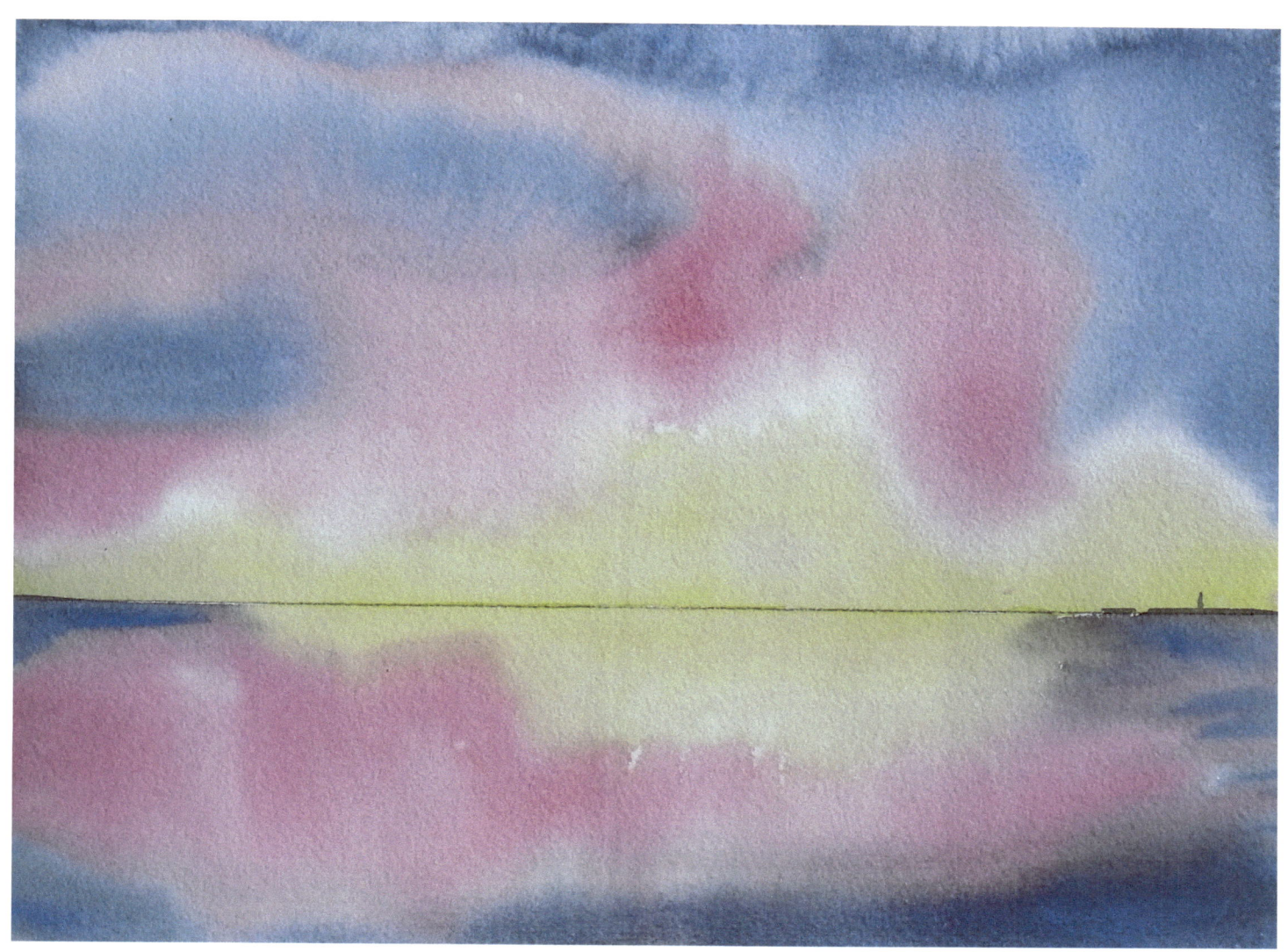

Early Morning Sun Andaman Sea

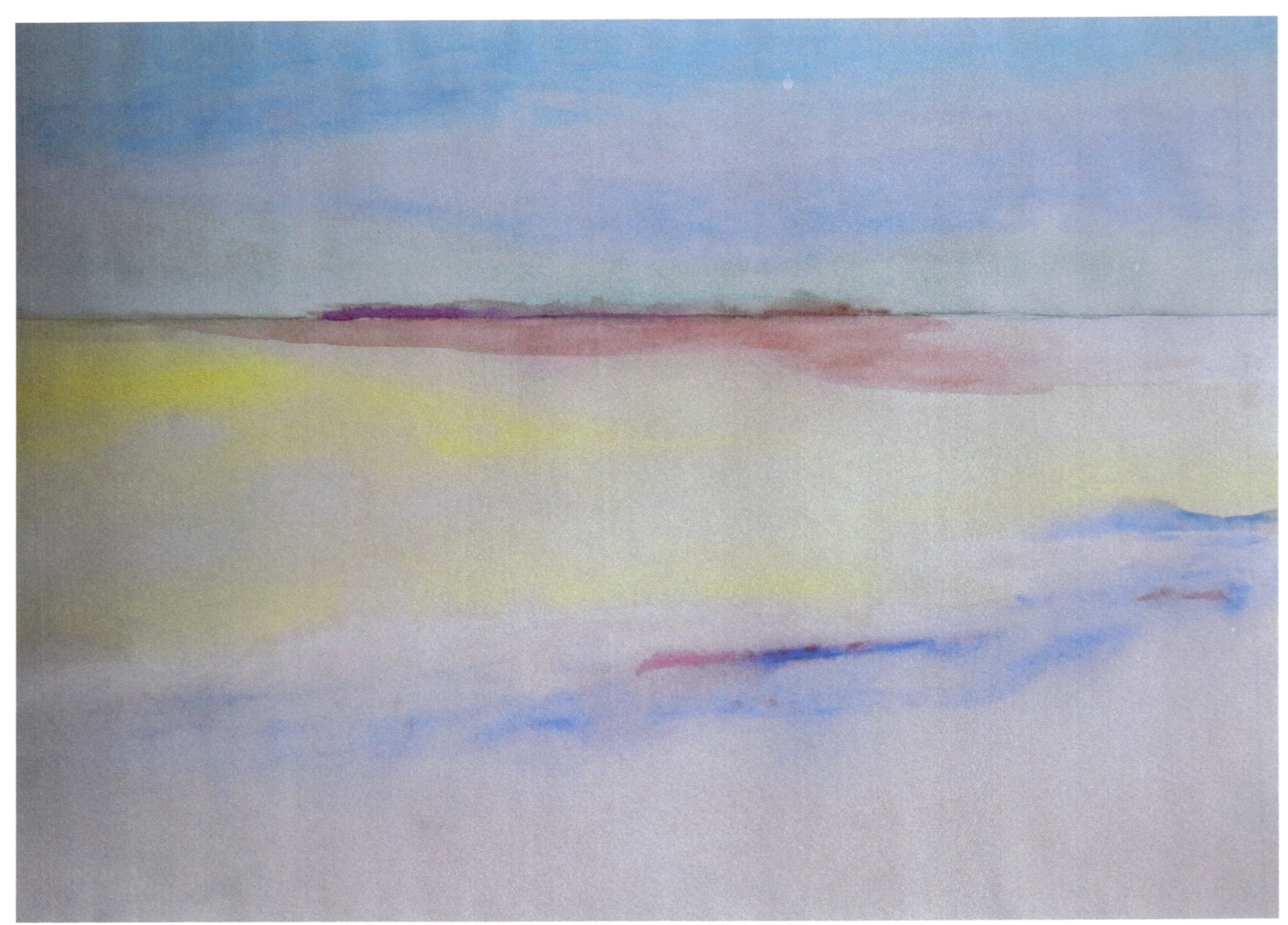

Still Tropical Sea

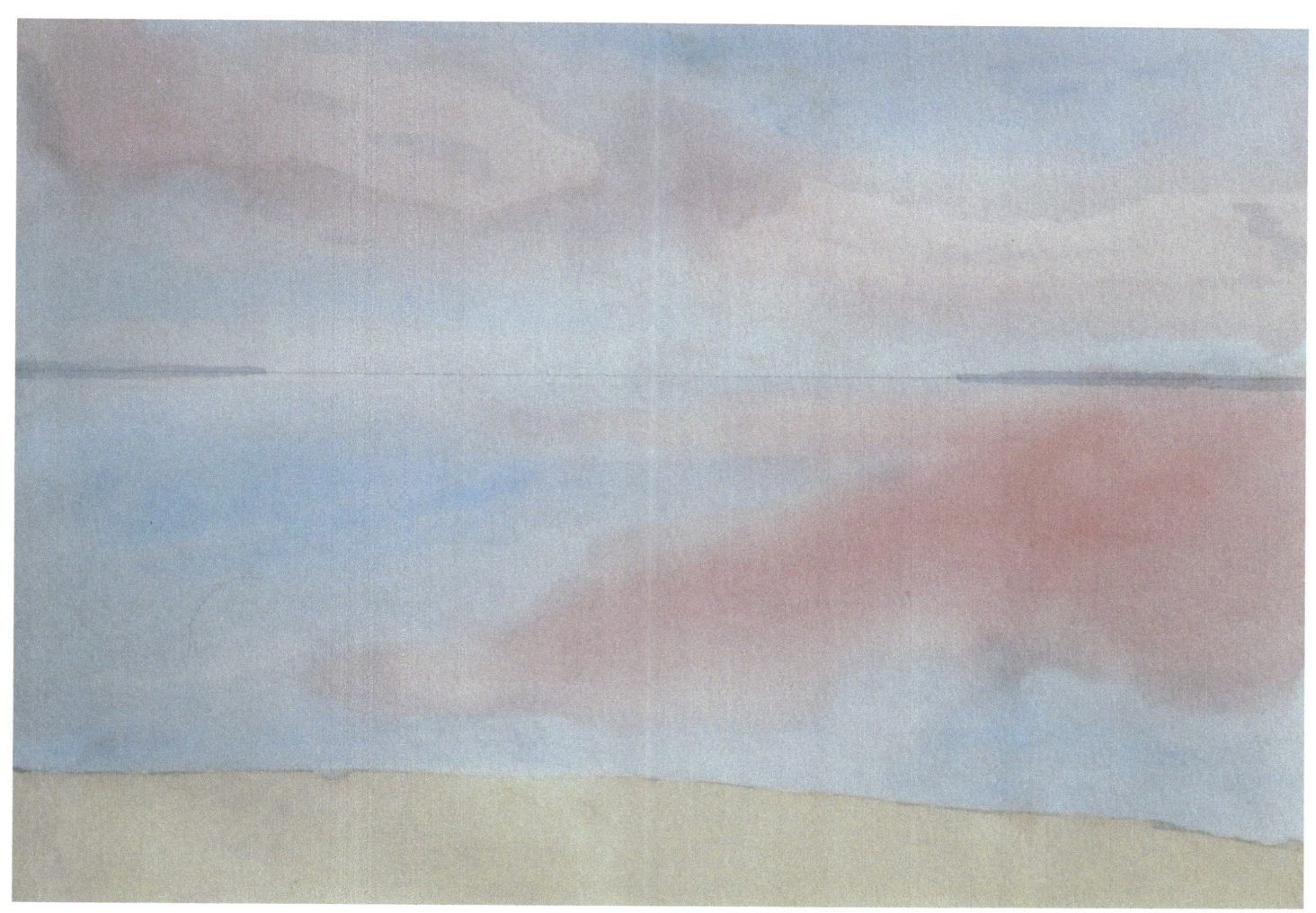

Sea Mist Penobscot Bay

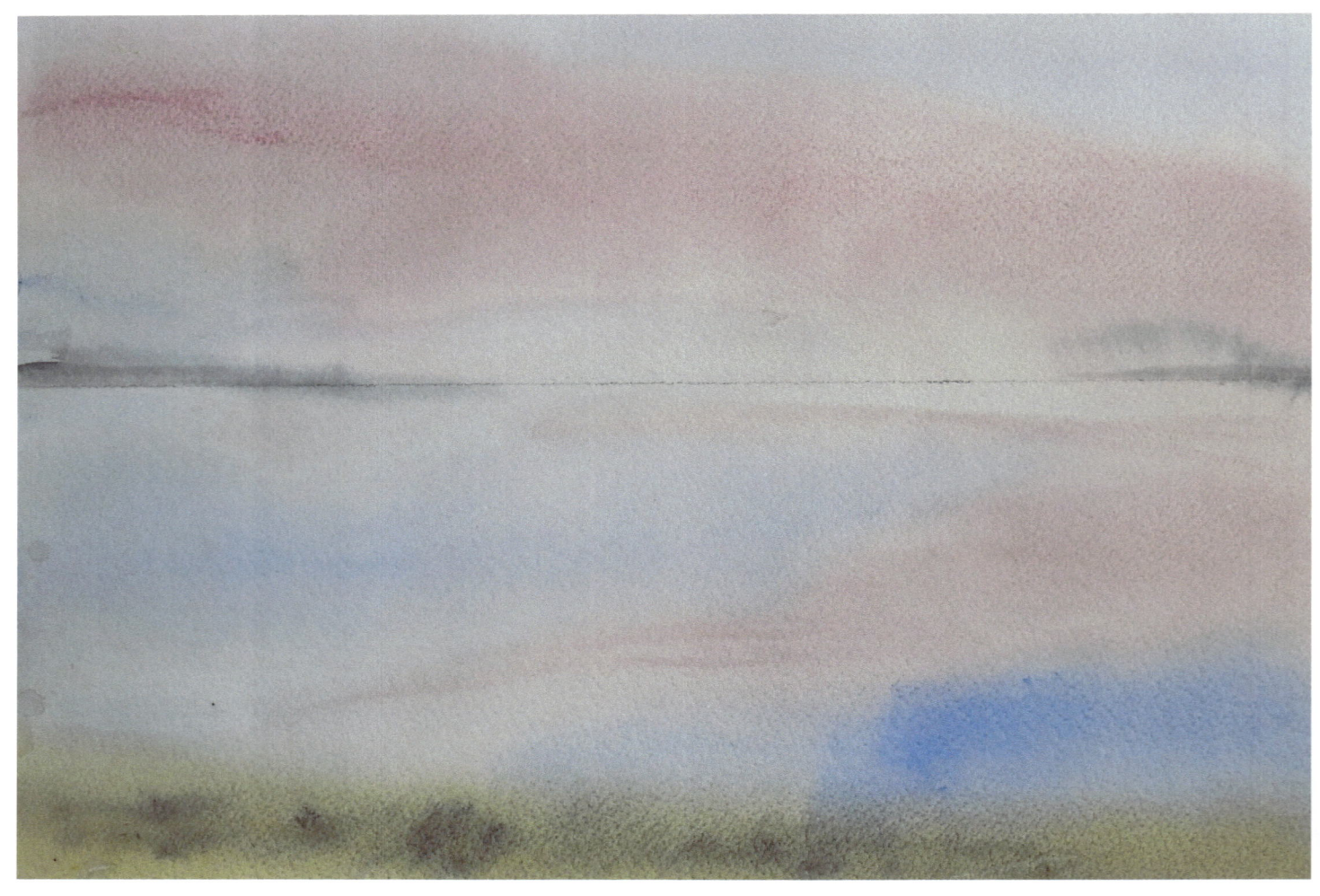

Misty Dawn Penobscot Bay

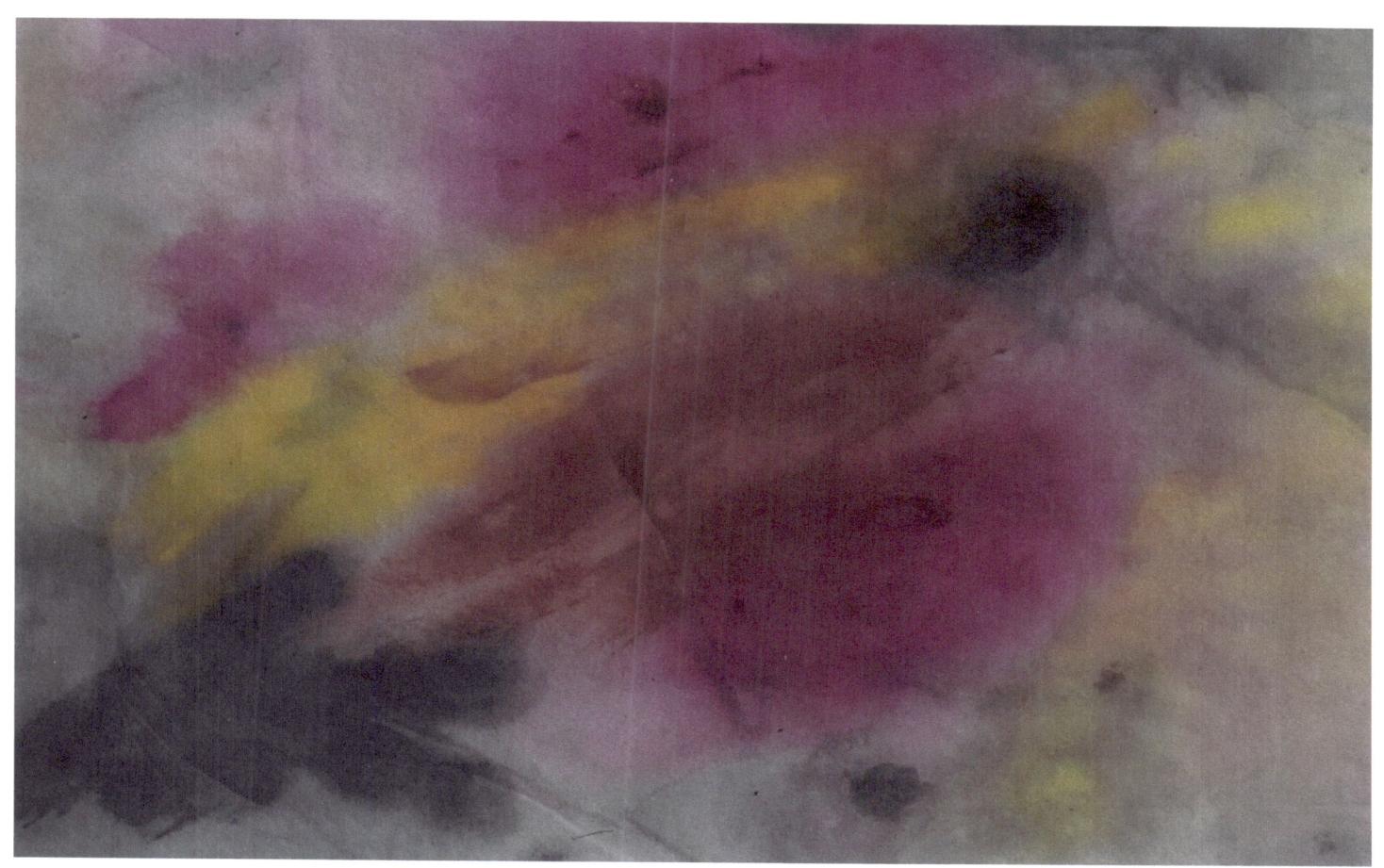

Summer Thunderstorm

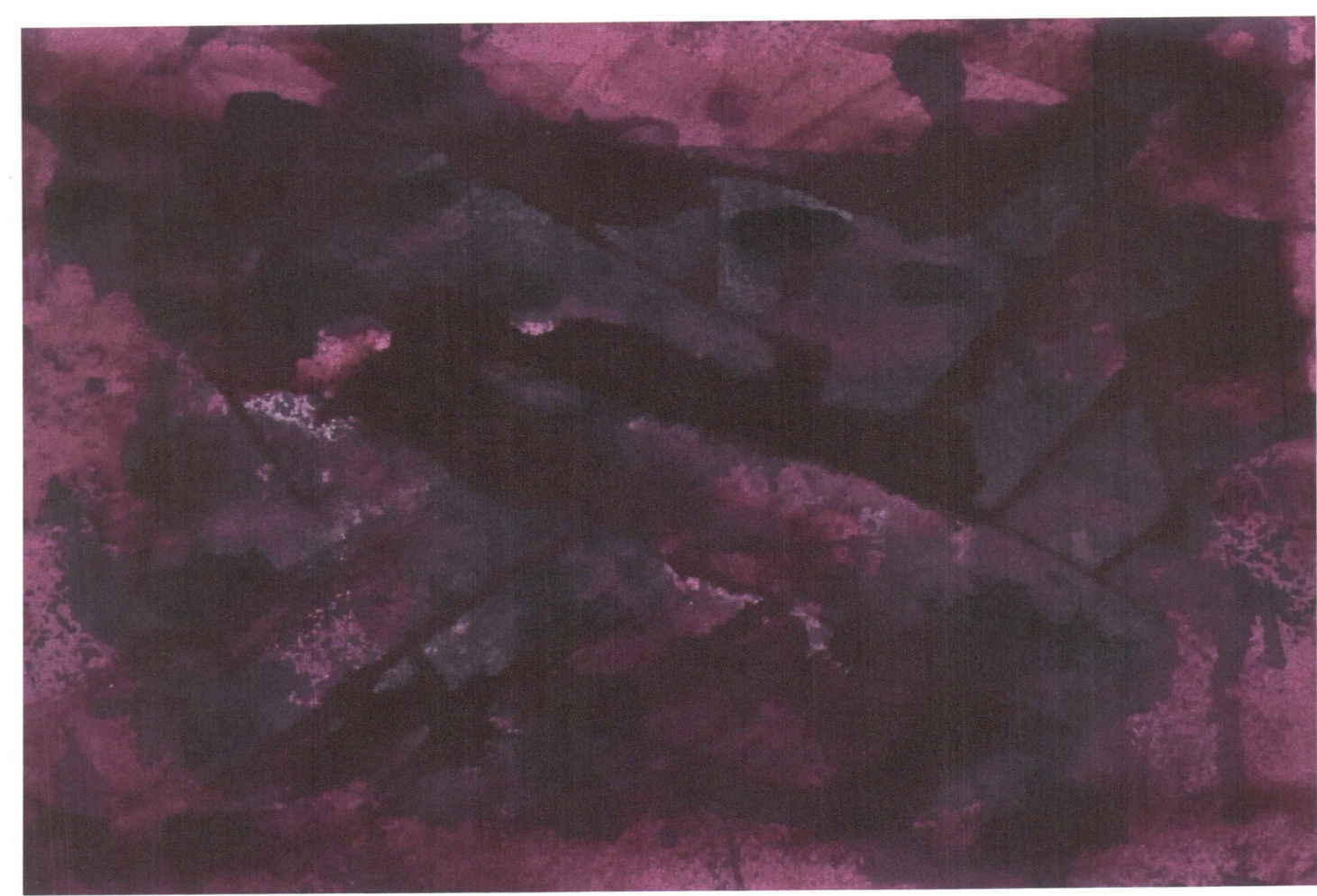

Turbulence

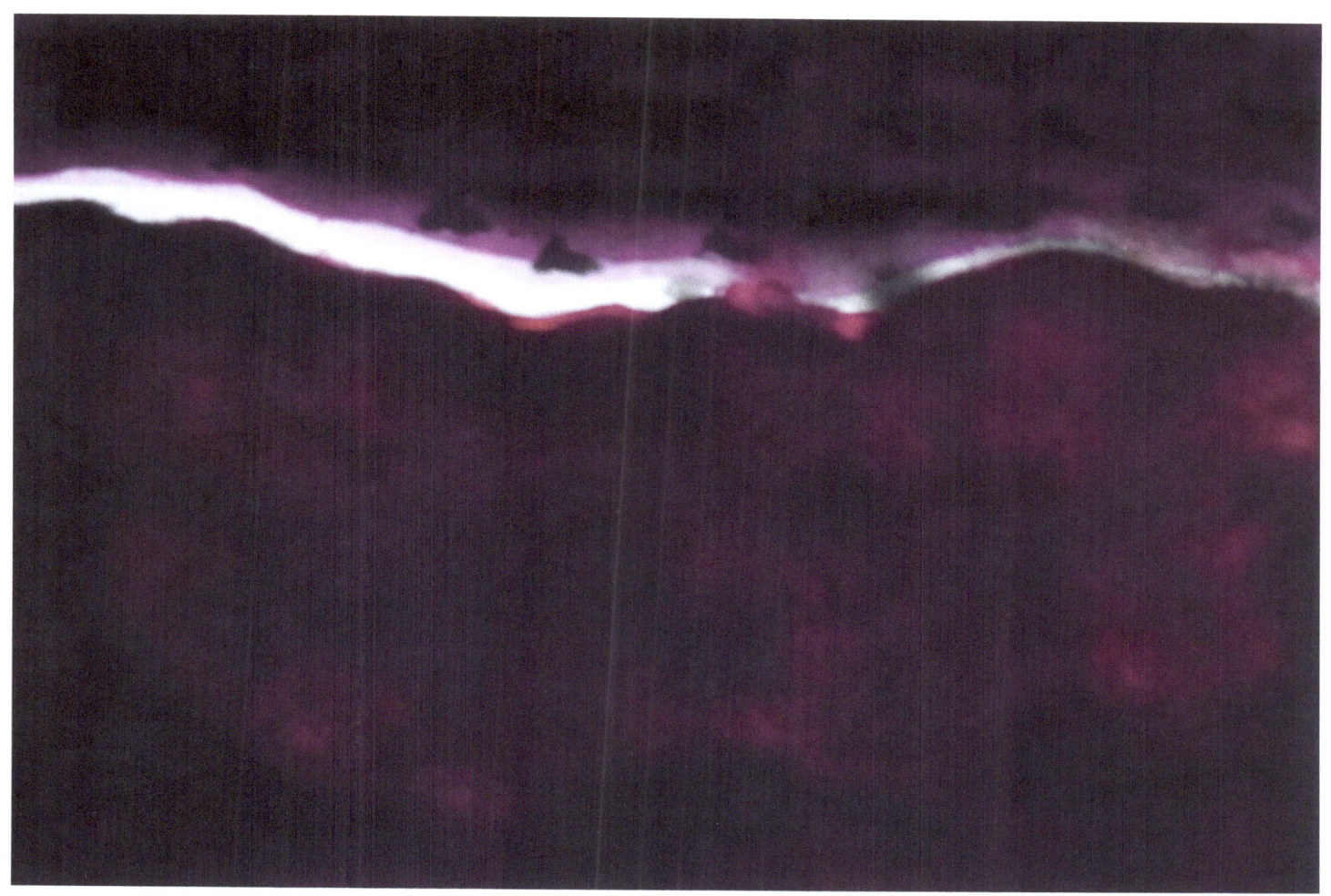

Mountain Dusk

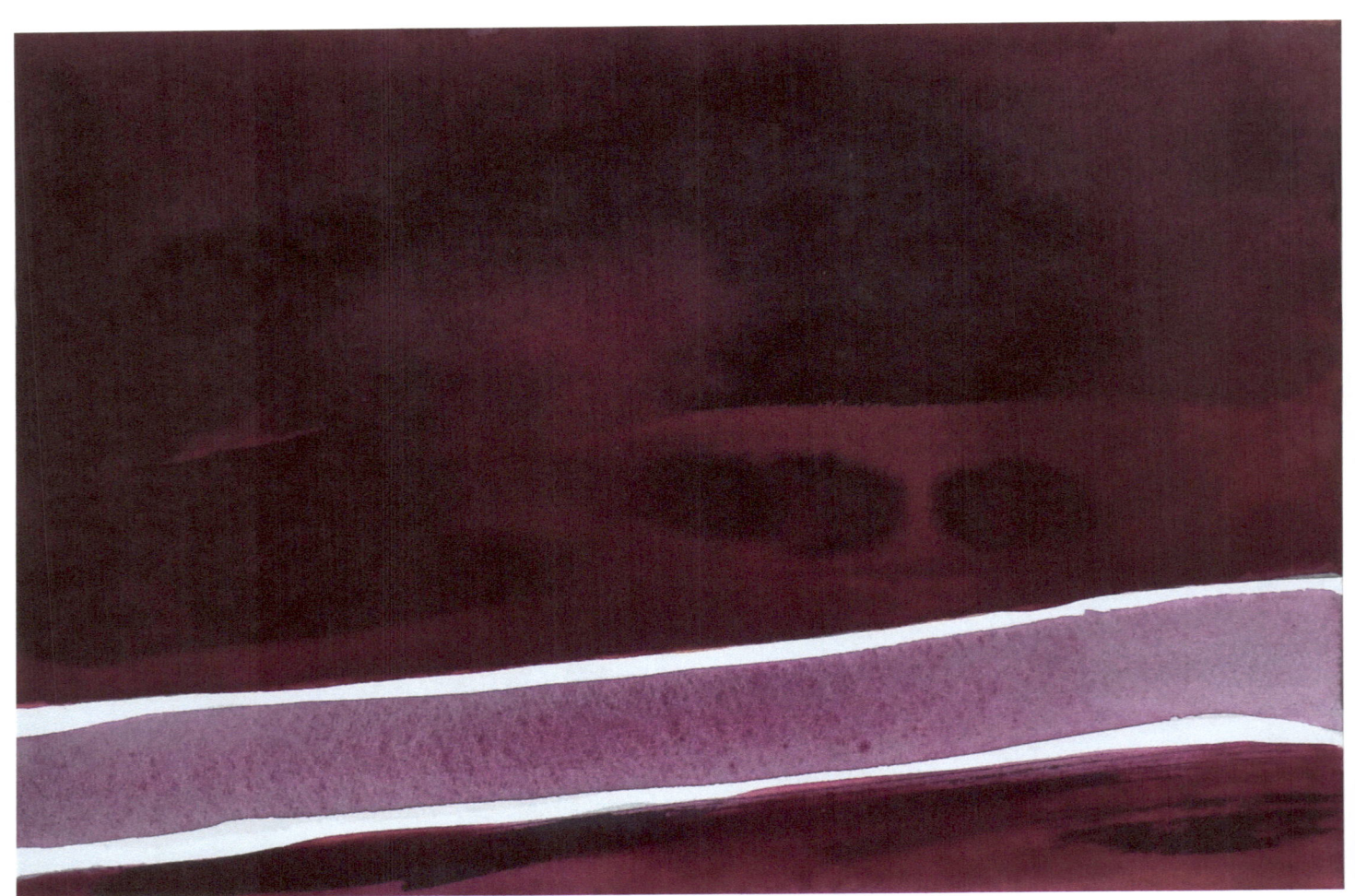

Mauve Pathway

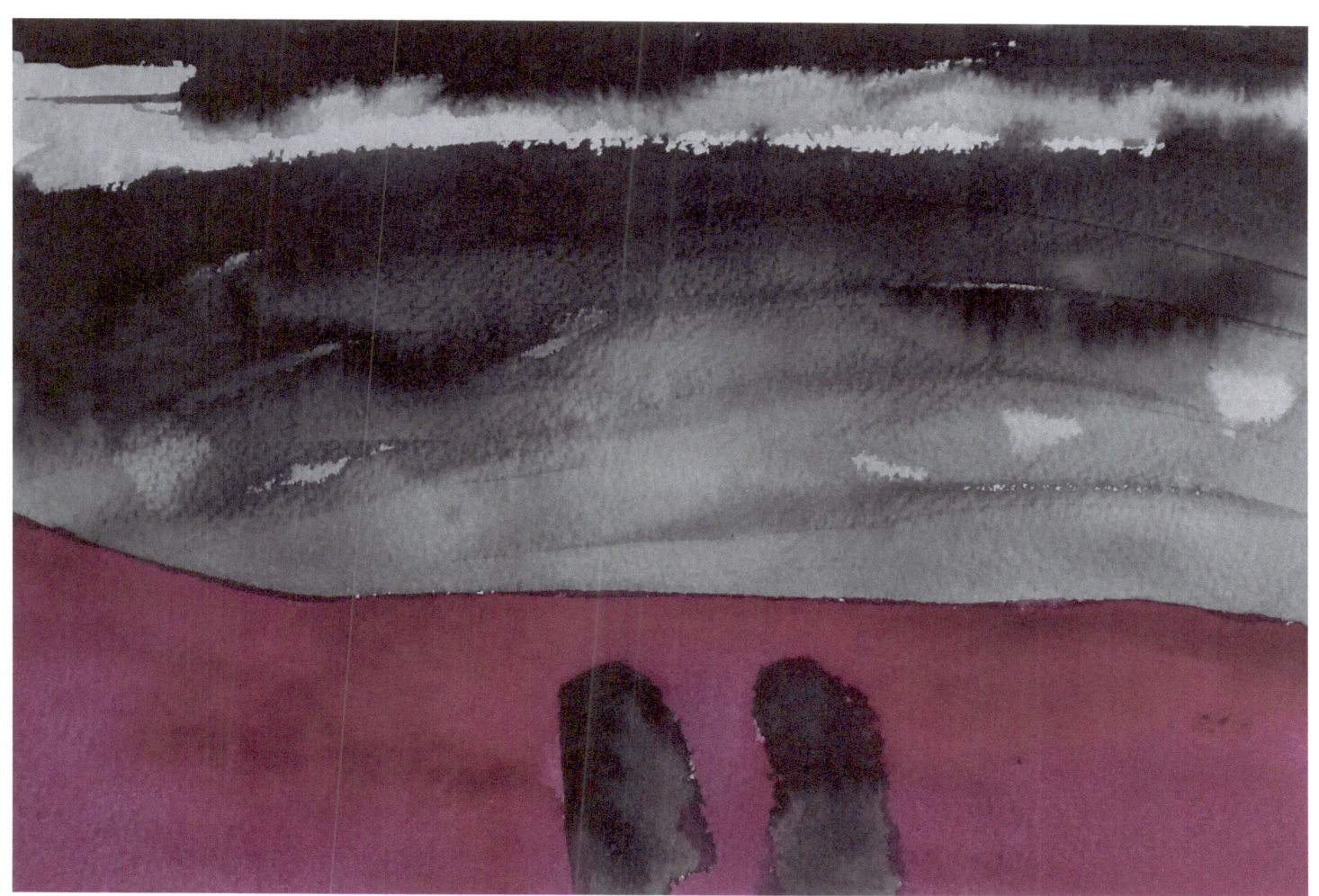

Approaching Storm

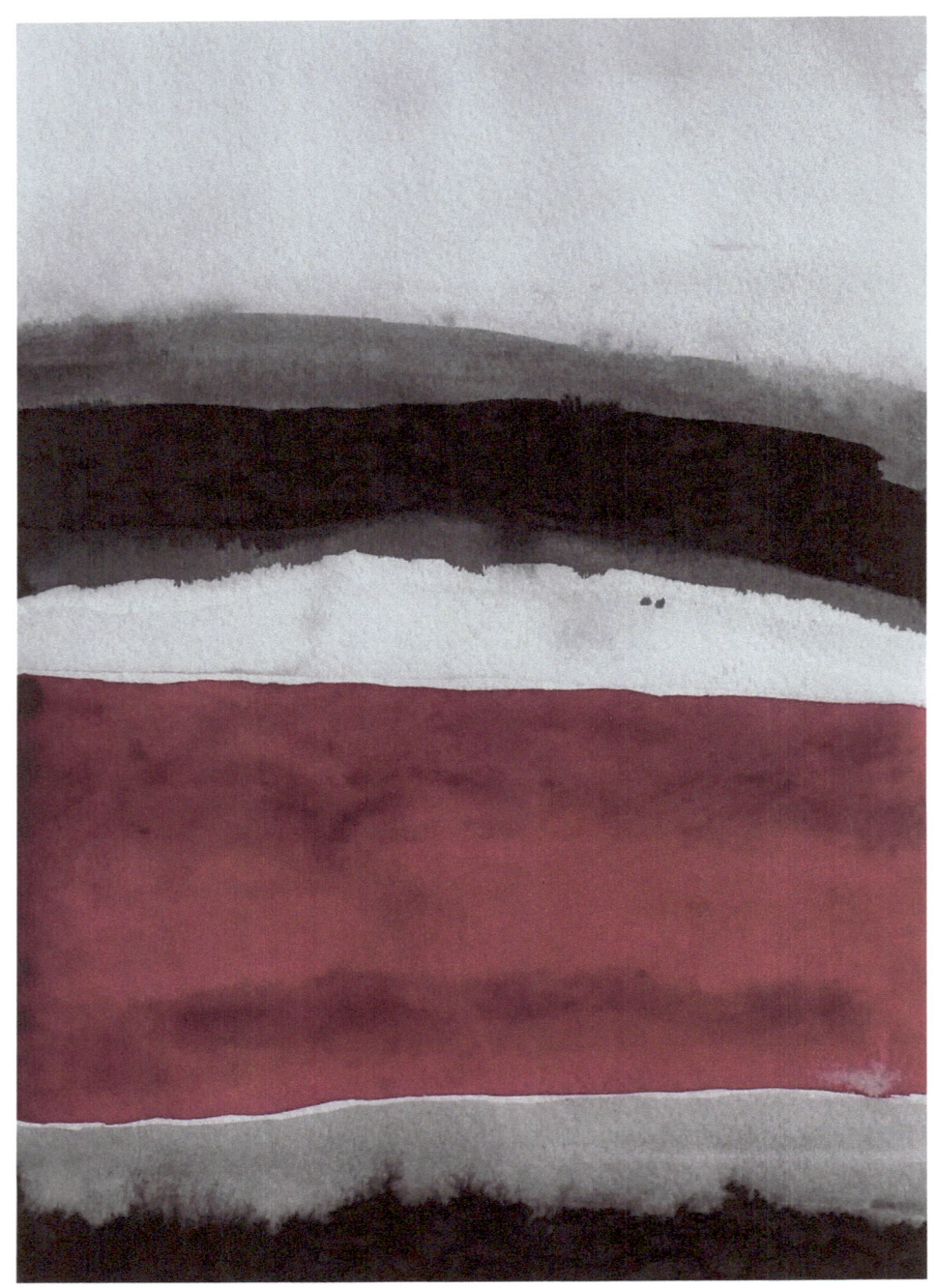

Ode to Rothko

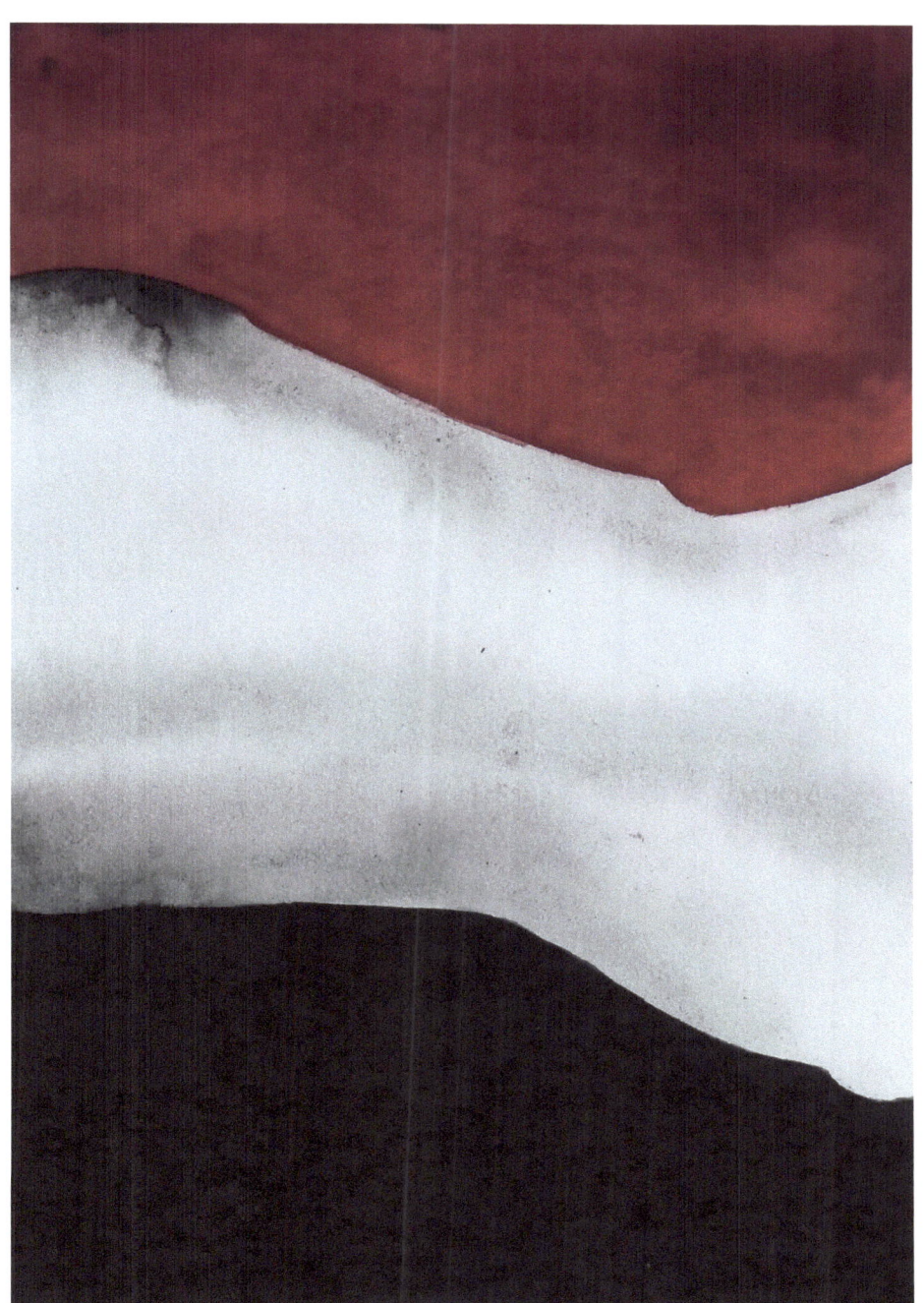

White Mountain Red Sky

Dawn Light Penobscot Bay

Red Mountain

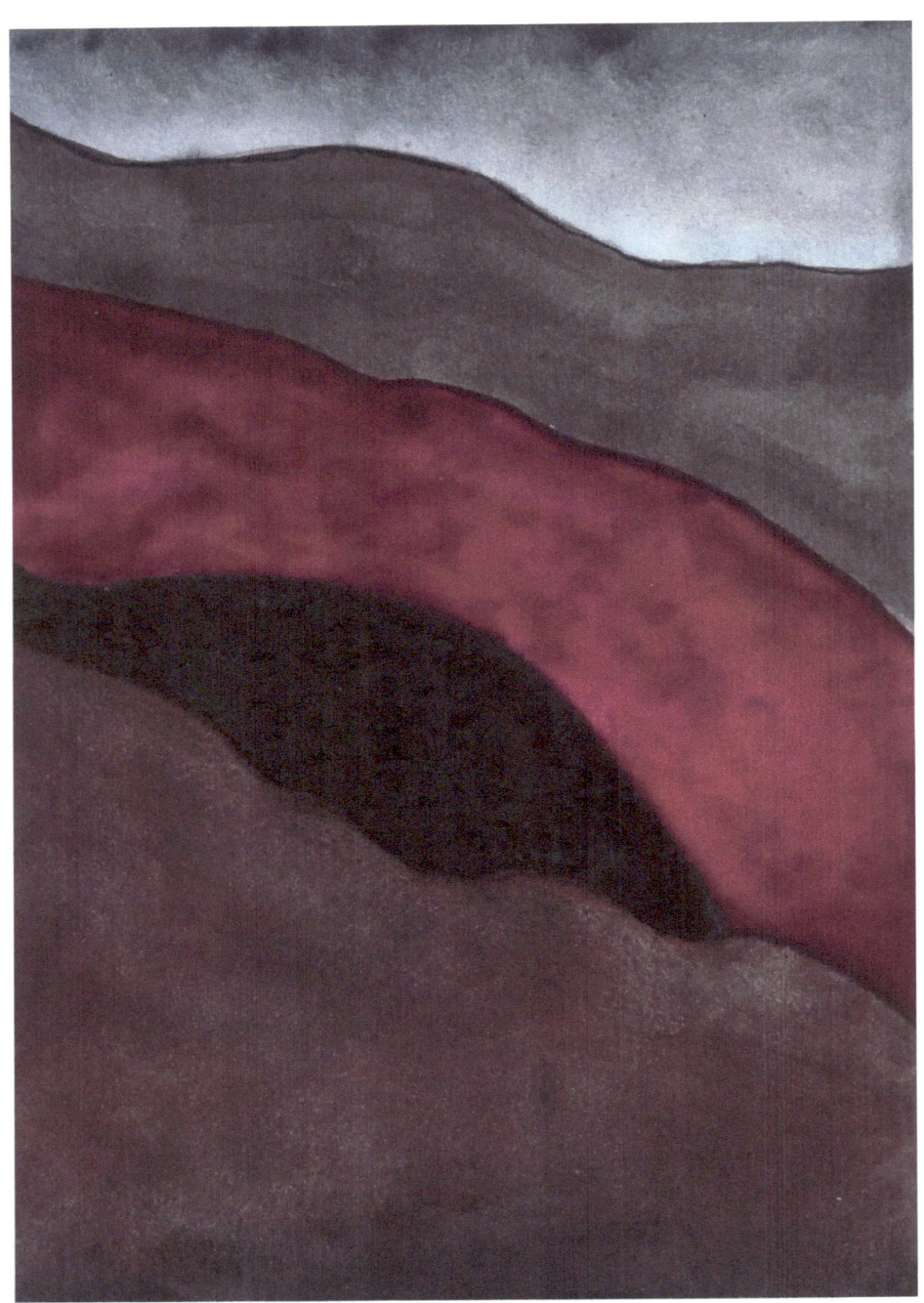

Dawn Light Penobscot Bay

Chris Coles Books

Bangkok Nights

Navigating the Bangkok Noir

Noir Nights in Phnom Penh

Team Trump Noir

Bangkok Noir in New York

One Night in Bangkok in Singapore

Kris Kolde in the Bangkok Night

Wintertime Santa Monica Beach

Intimate Landscapes

Seascapes Landscapes

Portraits from Bangkok

Patpong Portraits

Bangkok Noir in Pattaya

Colors of the Night

Portraits from the Bangkok Night

German Expressionism and the Bangkok Night

Night Visions

Bangkok Noir at Check Inn 99

Flowers, One Butterfly and the Bangkok Night

Bangkok Neon

Paintings from the Phnom Penh Night

Chris Coles Shows

Bergamot Station - Santas Monica 2005

Fritto Misto - Santa Monica 2006

Main Street Gallery - Santa Monica 2006

Agora Gallery - New York 2006

HHLT Gallery - Harpswell 2008

4th Street Gallery - Singapore 2009

Liam's Gallery - Pattaya 2009

Koi Gallery - Bangkok 2011

Bed Supperclub - Bangkok 2011

71 Prakanong - Bangkok 2011

FCCT - Bangkok 2012

Meta House Gallery - Phnom Penh 2013

Check Inn 99 - Bangkok 2015

Brainwake - Bangkok 2016

Check Inn 99 - Bangkok 2018

Meta House - Phnom Penh 2019

Hops Gallery - Phnom Penh 2019

www.ingramcontent.com/pod-product-compliance
Lightning Source LLC
Chambersburg PA
CBHW050807180526
45159CB00004B/1580